MY 26 '93

DISCARDED

D0342817

COLORADO MOUNTAIN COLLEGE   SP   Painter, Sidney,
CR4   French chivalry :

1 03 0000010126

cover stains noted 6/2021

CR   PAINTER, SIDNEY
4529   French Chivalry
F8
P3

OLORADO MOUNTAIN COLLEGE--LRC--WEST

S

FRENCH CHIVALRY

Chivalric Ideas and Practices in
Mediaeval France

LONDON: HUMPHREY MILFORD
OXFORD UNIVERSITY PRESS

PARIS: LIBRAIRIE E. DROZ

FRENCH CHIVALRY

Chivalric Ideas and Practices in Mediaeval France

By

SIDNEY PAINTER

BALTIMORE

THE JOHNS HOPKINS PRESS

Copyright 1940, The Johns Hopkins Press
Baltimore, Maryland 21218

Printed in the United States of America

Library of Congress Catalog Card Number 40–8951

Originally published, 1940
Second printing, 1951
Third printing, 1961
Fourth printing, 1966

To
N. F. P.

PREFACE

HAD not my colleagues persuaded me that the term essay is no longer used in the sense of an exploration into a wide and complicated field, I would have entitled this book *An essay on chivalric ideas and practices in mediaeval France.* Chivalry has long interested me as a subject for both social history and the history of ideas. I have attempted to deal with it from these two points of view.

The nature of the subject and the material used has made it impracticable to follow the established methodology of historical scholarship. The foot-notes are for the most part simply references to enable the reader to find the sources of direct and indirect quotations. They are intended to provide illustrations rather than proofs. Thus when I state that a certain idea was frequently found in troubadour poetry, I furnish an illustration of its use, but make no attempt to cite all the places where I have found it.

The first chapter entitled *The nobles of France* is not an integral part of the book. It is intended to provide for the reader who is not familiar with mediaeval history the background required for understanding the chapters on chivalry. The mediaeval historian would do well to start with the second chapter.

In general the foot-notes indicate my obligations to fellow scholars, but in three cases the recognition is most inadequate. The first chapter owes much to M. Marc Bloch's highly important work *Les caractères originaux de l'histoire rurale française* which contains an invalu-

able account of the economic history of the feudal class.
M. Léon Gautier's book *La chevalerie* is mentioned in
my notes, but I fail to state that a fair part of the material
I have used was found through looking up references
given by him. I am under peculiarly heavy obligations
to Mr. Raymond L. Kilgour whose *Decline of chivalry
as shown in the French literature of the late Middle
Ages* was of great service to me. Mr. Kilgour's summary
of the literature of the fourteenth and fifteenth century
was an invaluable guide through a vast mass of material.

Finally I wish to express my gratitude to the Johns
Hopkins Historical Seminar for the time and energy it
devoted to several of my chapters and to my friends who
read all or part of the manuscript and assisted me
through their criticisms. Professor Leo Spitzer of the
Johns Hopkins University read the fourth chapter and
Professors K. R. Greenfield and F. C. Lane of the same
University read the entire manuscript as did Professors
Grace Frank of Bryn Mawr College and John La Monte
of the University of Cincinnati. These scholars are in
no way responsible for my errors of commission or
omission, but both types would have been far more
numerous without their aid.

SIDNEY PAINTER

The Johns Hopkins University

CONTENTS

I

THE NOBLES OF FRANCE

CHIVALRY as we use the term denotes the ideals and practices considered suitable for a noble. The word itself is reminiscent of the milieu in which the ideas connected with it took shape—the aristocratic society of mediaeval France dominated by mounted warriors or *chevaliers*. As early as the eleventh century several sets of ideas appeared which represented different views of chivalric standards and behavior. During the next four hundred years these conceptions of the ideal nobleman were developed by and for the feudal class under the influence of a changing environment, intellectual, political, and economic. Hence it is necessary first of all to state very briefly the position of the noble class in the eleventh century and review the most important changes made in its status during the remainder of the Middle Ages.

Inheritance and environment had combined to give the nobles of eleventh-century France the personal characteristics of fierce, undisciplined, warrior chieftains. The Frankish aristocrats and the Saxon and Viking raiders had passed on to their descendants the pride, warlikeness, scorn of peaceful pursuits, impatience with restraint, and extreme individualism which had marked the wild Teutonic barbarian. These qualities in the noble strain had been strengthened by the events of the ninth and tenth centuries. The modicum of political restraint which the Frankish kings had imposed on their aristocracy disappeared with the collapse of the Carolingian monarchy. Although the development of the feudal hierarchy in the tenth century placed some limits on the independence of the lesser aristocrats, in general the growth of feudalism stabilized in a system of institutions the political results of royal weakness and noble usurpation. Moreover the continuous warfare that marked the period confirmed the bellicose tendencies of the aristocracy. While royal princes and great lords fought for the rather academic honor of being called king of a realm devastated by Viking raids, each noble waged war on his neighbor whenever he saw fit. Arrogance, hatred of restraint, and love of battle were bred into the very bone of the eleventh-century French nobility.

These feudal aristocrats who were so well endowed with the personal qualities appropriate to warriors were favored by contemporary tactical and economic conditions to such an extent that they had a complete monopoly of the military profession. The only type of soldier that was considered reasonably effective during the ninth, tenth, and eleventh centuries was the mounted warrior armed with helmet, hauberk, shield, sword, and lance. This equipment was so costly that it could be provided only by men of wealth, and its efficient use required rigid training from early youth and continuous practice throughout the soldier's active life. Hence the noble endowed with wealth and freedom from the necessity of working for his living was the only effective soldier. The fundamental importance of this monopoly of the profession of arms is shown by contemporary terminology. By the beginning of the eleventh century the various vague terms which had been used to designate the aristocrat had been supplanted by that of *miles*, soldier. The social and political nobleman had become completely identified with the fully armed warrior. With the exception of nobly-born members of the clergy, an adult male who was not a *miles* was not a noble.

The *miles* or knight was the master of eleventh-century France. His absolute power over the mass of the population was sanctioned by both tradition and force. For over two centuries the governmental authority wielded by the Frankish kings as successors to Imperial Rome had been dispersed among the knightly members of the feudal hierarchy. Time had sanctified the usurpations of royal power that formed the basis for seignorial jurisdiction. As long as the nobles held their monopoly of the military profession, rebellion against their authority was futile. The short-bow was the best weapon possessed by the lower classes, but its shafts were of little effect against knightly armor. Even if a peasant could find the means to procure the equipment of a knight, he would lack the training required to use it effectively. Until the non-noble class obtained wealth, leisure, or a cheap, easily used, and effective weapon, the position of the feudal aristocracy was perfectly secure.

The knights were supplied with their livelihood by the non-noble laymen, the serfs or villains, who lived on their estates. Whatever surplus the laboring class produced above the barest needs of subsistence went to their knightly lords. But as commerce was practically non-existent and little money was in circulation, this

surplus was not in a negotiable form. The serfs cultivated the knight's demesnes and paid him rents in
services and kind. The produce of the demesnes and
rents supplied food for the lord and his household. The
services of the serfs furnished labor for building the
lord's house and making his clothes. The spaciousness
and strength of a knight's residence and the size and
quality of his wardrobe were determined by the skill of
his serfs and the time they could spare from their work
in the fields. With the possible exception of military
equipment and occasional pieces of fine raiment everything the lord possessed was the product of the labor of
his own tenants.

In all probability the ordinary noble did not have
sufficient resources to live in a style which one could
call luxurious. Since mediaeval agricultural technique
was very inefficient, the individual peasant had little
surplus of time or produce. At the beginning of the
eleventh century the population of France was thin and
widely scattered, and a large part of the realm was
covered with forests. Two centuries of foreign invasion
and domestic anarchy had brought about the abandon-
ment of much of the land which had been cultivated
in the Carolingian period. As a result most knights had
few tenants in comparison to the extent of their fiefs.
But even when a lord had at his disposal a large supply
of serf labor, it must have been extremely unskilled.
The petty noble was obliged to be content with coarse
woolen clothes, great abundance of very simple food,
and a two-room wooden house surrounded by a moat
and palisade. A great lord might have enough serf
labor available to build a high artificial mound on

which to erect his residence. He might even have servile artisans who by specialization had learned to produce clothes and arms of reasonably good quality. Further he could not go. Fine stone castles, silken raiment, and spices had to await the reappearance of merchants and the money to hire skilled labor.

The necessary minimum of military and political cooperation between the nobles was provided for by the feudal system. It would be difficult to conceive of a more democratic form of government. The relations between a lord and his vassals were governed by customary regulations which were interpreted and enforced by the lord's court, a general assembly of the vassals presided over by the lord. This arrangement grew naturally out of the circumstances of the times. Force must be the ultimate sanction in all forms of government, and the force which was at the lord's disposal consisted of the armed levy of his vassals. As the vassals were extremely jealous of their independence, the restrictions on individual liberty imposed by the feudal system were as light as military necessity would permit. The vassal was obliged to obey his lord's summons to war. When the noble needed advice or a decision in a dispute concerning feudal custom, his vassals were bound to assemble at his call. As marriages were a popular way of creating alliances between noble houses, neither lord nor vassal could marry without the other's approval. But aside from matters which were of vital interest to the military organization of which he was a part the vassal was completely independent. The feudal system simply placed a few necessary restrictions on his relations with his lord, his fellow vassals, and their noble friends and foes. He could act as he pleased toward his non-noble subjects and his fellow knights in general.

The nobles who occupied the higher ranks of the feudal hierarchy found the limitations on their independence particularly slight. The simple knight who had neither vassals of his own nor a fortress stronger than a moated manor house was obliged to conform to the customs of the fief as interpreted by his lord and fellow vassals. If he flagrantly violated his feudal obligations, his lord could punish him. But the knight who ranked as a baron was in a much stronger position. He had a castle which could only be reduced by a long and exhausting siege, and his feudal levy might well be as large if not actually larger than his overlord's. Suppose for instance that a baron had twenty knightly vassals. His overlord was a count who had as his vassals twenty barons. In many parts of France these two nobles would find themselves with equal feudal levies. In short, while in some advanced feudal states such as the duchy of Normandy a vassal's military obligation to his lord was proportionate with the size of his fief, in most districts each fief no matter how important owed the service of a single knight. Even in Normandy the baron's obligation to the duke was unlikely to represent more than a fifth of his actual military resources. The eleventh-century baron who possessed a strong castle and a fair-sized band of vassals could often defy his lord with comparative impunity. If he was unable to resist his lord's host in the field, he could retire to his castle. As feudal levies served only for a limited time, usually forty days, a reasonably strong castle was practically impregnable. Only some outrageous act that thoroughly aroused his lord and his fellow vassals could seriously endanger the baron.

The eleventh-century French knight lived in a society which was dominated by force and in which competition by means of force was almost completely untrammeled. If a knight wished to increase his power and resources, he waged war on his neighbors. A successful raid was certain to produce plunder in the form of corn and cattle. A victory in a skirmish might result in the capture of horses and knightly prisoners who could be held for ransom. The capture of a baron of some importance could easily make the fortune of a poor knight. Villages, acres of good farm land, and even strong castles often changed hands to ransom a prisoner. Ability as a warrior was the chief quality needed by a knight. A weak lord might see a great fief which had been patiently built up by three generations of effective soldiers disintegrate in a few years. The hardiest fighters were eagerly sought by feudal princes with fiefs to bestow and fathers with daughters to marry. As in all free competition the fit survived and the unfit lost their property and disappeared, usually into a monastery. The noble was bred for war, trained for war, and passed his life fighting. He fought for amusement, for profit, and from a sense of duty.

In the last few pages I have attempted to describe the situation held by the feudal class in eleventh-century France. But civilization never stands still. The next four centuries saw important changes effected in the economic, political, military and social positions of the French nobility. The aristocracy grew richer, then poorer; it lost its political and military monopolies; rivals threatened its social dominance. As all these changes affected, or may well have affected, the ideals of the noble class and the extent to which those ideals were carried out in practice, they deserve the attention of the student of chivalry.

The first stage in the enrichment of the feudal class was brought about by an external and internal expansion of French society that began before the close of the eleventh century. The external phase of this expansion took the usual form of foreign conquest. French knights went on crusades to Spain and the Holy Land and invaded Sicily, southern Italy, and England. By the end of the century the passes over both the Tweed and the Jordan were watched by French warriors. The effect of these adventures on the fortunes of individual nobles varied widely. The younger son who won a rich fief in England, Sicily, or Syria was well repaid for his efforts, but many a crusader bankrupted himself in the holy cause. It seems reasonably certain, however, that the results of these expeditions were beneficial to the French nobility as a whole. The removal of the most adventurous and warlike members of the feudal class made less bitter the competition for French fiefs. Instead of attempting to oust his elder brother or plunder a neighbor the cadet of a noble house could seek his fortune in England or Palestine. The younger and bastard sons of the ducal house of Brittany carved out for themselves the great barony of Richmond in England. The Hauteville brothers left Normandy to found the Norman kingdom of Sicily. In the twelfth century the Poitevin house of Lusignan first stole everything available in Poitou and then turned their attention to the East where

Cyprus became their permanent domain and the Kingdom of Jerusalem long acknowledged their rule. The
emigration of these turbulent knights did not make
France peaceful, but it must have decidedly alleviated
the fierce struggle for existence among the nobles.

While the internal expansion of French society which
began in the eleventh century was much less spectacular
than the external, its effect on the noble class was just
as significant and probably more permanent. In its
earlier stages this internal expansion consisted of a broad
general colonization of land which had been deserted
during the ninth and tenth centuries. Later marshes
were drained and less easily cultivable waste put under
the plow. By the twelfth century the peasant pioneers
were nibbling at the edges of the vast forests. This
great colonization movement reached its height in the
twelfth century and had run its course by the middle of
the thirteenth. Its extent and importance is attested by
the map of France where one finds scattered over the
land places called Villeneuve, Neuville, or by some even
more expressive designation such as Les Essarts-le-Roi.
The effect of this expansion of arable land on the
position of the nobles is most obvious in those regions
where there were vast tracts of forest and waste. During
the twelfth and thirteenth centuries the duke of Brittany's demesne in the county of Rennes and the baronies
of Vitré and Fougères profited immensely from the
clearing of large parts of the forest of Rennes. The
duke's lordship of St. Aubin-du-Cormier was carved out
of the very heart of the forest. Every new settlement,
every acre of land brought under the plow meant added
resources for some member of the feudal class. For the

nobles as a whole it meant stronger residences and the
ability to feed and clothe larger households. M. Alfred
Jeanroy suggests that this increase in the resources of the
nobles had much to do with the appearance of troubadour poetry. Certainly it is an interesting coincidence
that the development of French literature should take
place while this expansion of the resources of the aristocracy was under way.

As long as the incomes of the nobles consisted almost
entirely of rents paid in services and kind, their expansion was of rather limited importance. The knight
had at his command a larger supply of labor and raw
materials, but the former did not increase in skill nor
the latter in quality or variety. Only the reappearance
of a money economy would permit the nobles to utilize
their revenues to provide for themselves a decidedly
more luxurious standard of living. This fundamental
change in the economic structure of France began in
the early twelfth century. Towns and fairs appeared;
local and inter-regional commerce began to develop.
While it was to be a long time before the nobles could
collect money rents from their peasants, the growth of
trade gave them many opportunities to obtain cash
revenues. The petty lord of a single manor began to
draw an income from market tolls and from dues as-
sessed against passing merchants. The baron of some
importance could see his purse bulging with the rents
of a town or two, while the great feudal potentate
would enjoy a princely income from international fairs
and flourishing cities. The feudal class as a whole began
to command cash revenues, and its more fortunate
members became extremely rich. The nobles built fine

stone castles, wore costly silks from the East and rare
northern furs, drank rich wines, and added sugar and
spices to their menus. The household knight who
served a powerful lord could expect an occasional gift of
money in addition to his food, arms, and clothing. The
wandering minstrel might hope for silver as well as a
dinner in payment for amusing the baron.

Despite its pleasant immediate results the reappearance of a money economy was eventually to have disastrous effects on the wealth of the nobility. The superior
negotiability of cash and the inefficiency of obligatory
labor tempted the lords to commute the rents in kind
and services owed by their peasants into money pay-
ments. Meanwhile the continuous diminution of the
seignorial demesnes which had been in progress since
Carolingian times went on at an accelerated pace. It
was easier and more profitable for a lord to rent his
demesne than to attempt to farm it through agents. As
a result of these processes the nobles tended to become
landlords living on fixed money rents and so were extremely vulnerable to changes in the currency or in
prices. The extensive depreciation of the coinage carried
out by the French kings in the fourteenth and fifteenth
centuries seriously reduced the purchasing power of the
revenues of the aristocrats. The rapid rise in prices that
marked the sixteenth century almost ruined the nobility
of France.

The decline in the real value of the nobles' revenues
was not the sole cause of their impoverishment. The
second half of the Hundred Years War seriously im-
paired the wealth of the aristocrats. The long series of
English victories over the chivalry of France resulted in

the reduction of the resources of many families through frequent payment of ransom. The chaotic condition of the king's government and the emptiness of his treasury must have forced the nobles to bear a large part of the costs of war. While theoretically they were captains in the king's pay, the money for themselves and their men was probably always far in arrears. They could, of course, recoup part of their losses by plundering and collecting ransoms from their prisoners, but the French countryside had been very thoroughly ravaged and the losing side gains few valuable captives. Moreover the nobles as landowners suffered indirectly from the depressed condition of the agricultural population. In most parts of France the ravages of armies and free companies had reduced the peasants to abject poverty. Villages stood deserted and fields lay untilled. The result of this general devastation was a serious diminution in the income of the landed proprietors.

Unfortunately the reduction in the revenues of the noble class was only half the difficulty. Ever since the thirteenth century the general development of European civilization had been gradually advancing the standards of luxurious living. By the second half of the fifteenth century graceful and comparatively spacious semi-defensible chateaux were beginning to replace the grim feudal fortresses. Rich, warm tapestries had supplanted painting in mural decoration. The articles of furniture required for comfortable living had increased in number and cost. Both clothes and food had become richer, more varied, and far more expensive. A nobleman was expected to dress in silks and rare furs. Jewelry was used extensively by both men and women. Such exotic

foods as sugar and oranges had become a necessary
feature of well appointed feasts. The passion of the
nobles for silver plate had become so keen that sumptuary legislation was passed in the hope of limiting this
source of extravagance. Finally the ideas and fashions
of the Italian Renaissance had begun to appear in
France, and some nobles were collecting great libraries
and even hiring Italian artists. In short the fifteenth
century saw not only a decrease in the income of the
nobles but also a decided increase in the cost of living
nobly.

The combination of reduced revenue with increased
expenses forced most nobles to seek additional sources
of income. Some tried to manage their estates more
profitably by recovering their dissipated demesnes and
becoming farmers as well as landlords. Others married
the richly endowed daughters of prosperous townsmen.
The majority, however, turned their eyes toward the
streams of gold which were flowing into the purses of
the more fortunate princes. The late fifteenth century
was a period of prosperity for the commerce and industry of France, and the lords who controlled important
towns collected their share of the profits. Drawn by this
golden magnet the nobles swarmed about the princes in
search of offices and pensions. The rebellious group of
aristocrats who organized the " League for the Public
Weal " against King Louis XI were primarily interested
in obtaining pensions and were remarkably successful in
their efforts. But only the more powerful nobles could
hope to extort pensions by force. Their fellows were
obliged to win rewards by service on the battle field or
in the household. While a noble who was endowed

with the traditional courage and hardihood of his class
could make a living in the army, a far more lucrative
course was to learn the art of pleasing princes—of being
a decorative, gay, witty, and amusing companion. Driven
by luxurious tastes and empty pockets the nobles of
France entered on their metamorphosis into courtiers.

Long before the reappearance of money economy
began to affect adversely the economic position of the
feudal class, it brought about a serious reduction in the
political power of the majority of the nobles. The
growth of towns and commerce increased the revenues
of the aristocracy as a whole, but the benefits were
not distributed evenly through the ranks. The feudal
princes like the Capetian kings, the dukes of Normandy,
and the counts of Champagne and Flanders profited far
more than the lesser lords. In general the rich revenues
of flourishing towns and fairs flowed into the pockets of
the princes. The highly lucrative fairs of Champagne
and the two chief towns of the district, Provins and
Troyes, were held in demesne by the counts of Champagne. The houses of Thouars and Lusignan were
masters of rural Poitou, but their overlord, the count of
Poitou, possessed the prosperous towns of Poitiers and
La Rochelle. In short the revival of trade tipped the
feudal balance in favor of the lords who occupied the
higher ranks in the hierarchy by giving them an increase
in resources out of all proportion to that enjoyed by their
vassals.

By the latter half of the twelfth century the money
revenues of many feudal princes were large enough to
permit them to begin to shake themselves free from the
political control exercised over their policies by their

vassals. Under the regime of barter economy a lord had
been absolutely dependent on the cooperation of his
vassals. They were the only soldiers available to him.
The constables and garrisons of the lord's castles, the
administrators of his outlying estates, and even the
officers of his household were drawn from the ranks of
his vassals. If a lord offended the majority of his vassals,
he might find himself without an army and see his own
castles held against him. In short the vassals acting in
unison could completely control their lord's political
policy. When in 1192 King Philip Augustus attempted
to invade Normandy in defiance of a papal prohibition,
his barons refused to follow him and so effectually frus-
trated his plans. Naturally the feudal princes were
anxious to free themselves from the control of their
vassals, and the possession of cash incomes enabled
them to do so. France was full of impecunious knights
who were glad to fight for pay. While it was not until
the latter years of the thirteenth century that the king
of France could afford to hire an army large enough for
a major campaign like the invasion of Normandy mentioned above, by the end of the twelfth he was relying
very largely on paid troops. The same policy was followed by his great vassals. When a feudal prince wished
to punish a contumacious vassal or conduct a minor raid
against a neighbor, he used a hired army. The same
money revenues which enabled the prince to have
mercenary soldiers permitted him to employ paid officials. His castellans became salaried officers in command
of garrisons of hired troops. The business of his court
and the administration of his estates were entrusted to
paid civil servants. The vassals who had been the only

agents and servants of the feudal princes were replaced
by professional administrators. Moreover this new group
of officials was in general drawn from the merchant
class. The townsman who owed his office entirely to
his lord's favor was far more tractable than the noble
steeped in the tradition of independence which characterized his class. The *baillis* of Philip Augustus were
either petty knights who hoped to rise in the royal
service or sons of merchants, while his minor officials
were almost all townsmen. Thus a lord's noble vassals
were no longer able to control his military policy by
refusing to serve in his host and were obliged to see men
of the middle class taking their places as his political
agents.

The lesser nobles not only lost much of their influence over their overlords' policies, but they also suffered
a diminution of their own political independence. The
ability to hire knights to fight for them and middle class
professional administrators to conduct the business of
their governments enabled the feudal princes to restrict
the sovereignty of their vassals and to build up centralized states. No longer were the princes obliged to use
agents whose political ideals and interests were identical
with those of their vassals. The middle class official
tended to bend all his efforts toward strengthening his
master's authority with little regard for the traditional
privileges of minor nobles. Moreover the recalcitrant
knight could no longer rely on the sympathy of his
fellow vassals who composed the lord's army or on the
forty-day limit set to the service of the feudal host. If
a prince had sufficient money and determination, he
could hire troops to invade the lands of a rebellious

vassal and reduce his castle by siege. By the middle of
the thirteenth century the Capetian kings and their
great vassals had become masters of their domains., The
duke of Brittany and the count of Champagne were
contractual feudal allies of the French kings, but they
ruled their own nobles as firmly as the kings governed
the lesser vassals of the crown.

During the fourteenth and fifteenth centuries this
process of centralization which was rapidly reducing
the political authority of the minor nobility was inter-
rupted. Early in the fourteenth century the nobles of
the royal domain united to extort from the sons of Philip
the Fair a series of charters guaranteeing them many
of the political privileges of which they had been deprived by Philip and his predecessors. A few years later
the outbreak of the Hundred Years War began a long
period of confusion which allowed the lesser nobles to
regain much of their independence. Although Charles
V was able to restore order and impose his authority on
the aristocracy, his efforts were nullified by the semi-
anarchy of the second half of the war. It was not until
the English had been driven finally from French soil
that the kings and the great princes could resume the
task begun by their predecessors in the thirteenth century. The end of the fifteenth century saw the vast
majority of the nobles reduced to the status of subjects
and deprived of all independent political authority.

From the point of view of the student of chivalry the
most important result of the development of centralized
feudal states in the twelfth and thirteenth centuries was
a decrease in the nobles' opportunities to follow their
traditional occupation—private war. No feudal prince

who had the power to prevent it was willing to see his fief laid waste by the interminable quarrels of his vassals. As early as the second half of the eleventh century King William the Conqueror placed many restrictions on private warfare in his duchy of Normandy. William's example was followed by his fellow princes as soon as they had developed their power sufficiently. By the end of the twelfth century private war between petty nobles was sternly discouraged in most parts of France and was apparently quite rare. The century between 1150 and 1250 was marked by wars between the great vassals of the crown and between the Plantagenet and Capetian monarchies. St. Louis and his immediate successors were strong enough to curb the turbulence of the feudal princes and to prohibit private war entirely. As a result by the end of the thirteenth century the right to wage war had become in theory and to a reasonable extent in practice a royal monopoly. The Hundred Years War was a prolonged struggle between the feudal monarchies of France and England. While this war consisted in large measure of a vast number of petty local campaigns, the nobles fought in the king's name against the king's enemies. Only at times of serious political confusion such as the periods following the French defeats at Poitiers and Agincourt did real private war become common. In short after the middle of the twelfth century a noble who wished to follow the traditional occupation of his class was obliged to do so under the authority of a feudal prince or feudal monarch.

Gradual and incomplete though it was the repression of private warfare had a significant effect on the function of the feudal aristocrat as a soldier. In the tenth and eleventh centuries the nobles had been military entrepreneurs. Within the very elastic limitations imposed by feudal custom each knight had used his own sword or his little band of vassals in whatever way seemed most profitable. He risked his horse, his arms, his freedom, and perhaps even his fief in the hope of gaining some material profit from his opponents. The most striking example of this sort of military enterprise on a large scale was the Norman conquest of England. William of Normandy and his knights were a group of adventurers bound together by the hope of making valuable conquests in the Anglo-Saxon realm. When success crowned their efforts, the profits were divided among the shareholders. The rise of the feudal princes tended to destroy the knight's status as an entrepreneur and turn him into an employee. The wars of the twelfth, thirteenth, and fourteenth centuries were fought in the interest of kings and princes. The knight was usually a hired soldier whose personal interests were not deeply involved. Moreover the risks and possibilities for profit were both limited. If a knight lost his horse or arms on a campaign, the prince was bound to repay him. If he were captured, the prince would usually pay part of his ransom. On the other hand the prince demanded a share of the ransoms of any prisoners taken by his knights and conquests in the form of castles and lands were his alone.

Although the commercial and urban revival with the attendant development of centralized feudal states changed the rôle of the nobles in war, only a revolution in contemporary tactics could seriously threaten their monopoly of the profession of arms. As long as the heavily armed horseman remained the only effective soldier, the feudal caste was secure in its position. Theoretically a feudal prince could have hired low-born men and trained and equipped them as knights, but the weight of tradition and the large number of nobles who were willing to serve for pay made so radical a course both difficult and unnecessary. The aristocracy maintained throughout the middle ages an almost complete monopoly of the cavalry of France. But an army composed of cavalry alone labored under definite tactical disadvantages, and continuous efforts were made to develop effective infantry. It was the partial success of these attempts that destroyed the absolute military monopoly of the nobles.

Even in the tenth and eleventh centuries there had been some non-noble troops who fought on foot. A warring baron would often bolster his feudal host with a levy of serfs. As these rustics had neither wealth to pay for equipment nor time to devote to training, they were of little or no value in battle. Their most effective weapon, the short-bow, was impotent against knightly armor. The only use that could be made of servile troops was to send them out to skirmish with the serfs of the opposing force as a prelude to the clash of the feudal horse. During the course of the twelfth century kings and feudal princes tried several methods of obtaining effective infantry. The Capetian kings turned their eyes toward the townsmen of their domains. The burgher had sufficient wealth to provide himself with decent equipment and he could find time for a modicum of training. Unfortunately the townsmen were unwarlike in their tastes and disliked devoting their time to drill and military service. While the communal militia of France became a useful auxiliary to the feudal host in such emergencies as the battle of Bouvines (1214), it resolutely refused to participate in extended campaigns and proved unable to withstand the noble cavalry in the open field. In general the townsmen could be relied on only for the defense of their own walled towns. In this capacity they formed an extremely important part of the military resources of the realm, but they did not compete with the nobles.

A far more successful means of acquiring a useful infantry force than levying serfs or townsmen was to hire, train, and equip mercenary troops. Towards the end of the twelfth century the development of the cross-bow gave the foot-soldier a missile weapon which could under favorable conditions pierce knightly armor. In the wars waged between Capetians and Plantagenets during the thirteenth century bands of crossbowmen played an important part in military tactics. While they could not withstand the feudal cavalry in the open field, when covered by knights or sheltered behind walls they could do great damage to the noble horsemen. The nobles were fully aware that the crossbow threatened their military monopoly. The chivalrously inclined writers of the twelfth and thirteenth centuries poured scorn on the heads of princes who made use of cross-bowmen. The church solemnly banned the weapon in wars between Christians. Moreover the noble generals of the day used these hated troops with so little tactical intelligence that the true value of their weapon was concealed. As a result while crossbowmen remained throughout the Middle Ages an important part of the

French military system, they were merely auxiliary troops and did not seriously threaten the tactical supremacy of the heavy noble cavalry.

Such changes in offensive weapons as the introduction of the crossbow in the twelfth century and of the English longbow in the fourteenth resulted in developments in knightly equipment which while they did not alter the position of the nobility as a whole, had interesting effects on its internal organization and terminology. In the eleventh century a knight's armor consisted of an open-faced helmet and a linen hauberk on which were sewn small metal disks. By the end of the twelfth century he was expected to have a great pot-helm which rested on his shoulders and covered his head and neck while his body was protected by a hauberk of chain mail. A century later many exposed parts of his body such as breast and thighs were covered by plate armor and his horse was at least partially mailed. By the fifteenth century the effectiveness of the longbow had caused both horse and man to be completely encased in plate armor. Each step in this development of knightly equipment increased its cost. As a result as time passed fewer and fewer members of the feudal class could afford to become knights. In the twelfth century every feudal male was a knight, but in the fifteenth the knights were an aristocratic minority of the nobles. The members of the feudal class who could not afford knightly equipment were obliged to serve in the army in the best armor they could buy. The feudal cavalry of the twelfth century was composed of men whose equipment was about the same. In the fifteenth century there was a wide divergence between the armor of the knight and of the poor noble who could afford only an open-faced helm and a chain-mail hauberk. The term squire which in the twelfth century usually marked the noble who was too young to be a knight came in time to designate the vast majority of nobles. This was, however, merely a change in terminology. The squire of the fifteenth century was socially, politically, and intellectually a noble even though he could rarely hope to become a knight.

The tactical revolution that was to deprive the noble cavalry of its overwhelmingly dominant position in the French military system came in the second half of the fifteenth century. Although Crécy, Poitiers, Agincourt, and many other battles had shown that the feudal horse and its tactics were no match for the English long-bowmen, the longbow never became established in France, and the heavy cavalry remained the backbone of the French army. But the rout of the chivalry of Burgundy by the Swiss pikemen heralded the appearance of infantry superior to any that the continent of Europe had produced during the Middle Ages. Drilled to maneuver in mass formation, the Swiss could withstand the charges of the heavy horse. Determined and well-led cavalry could impede and delay their advance, but could rarely stop them or destroy their mass formation. By the close of the fifteenth century Swiss mercenary pikemen were an important part of the French military system. During this same century artillery was developed which was suitable for use in the field. Although the cavalry could and usually did stay out of the range of these cumbersome early guns, the artillery deprived the heavy horseman of his chief tactical advantage—his comparative immunity from wounds. Defensive positions supplied with artillery were safe from his charges. Thus the fifteenth century saw the noble cavalry forced to share its place in the army with mercenary infantry and trains of artillery.

The changes in French civilization which had made such vital modifications in the economic, political, and military positions of the nobles during the four centuries between the years 1100 and 1500 also produced rivals who could threaten their social preëminence. In the eleventh century the structure of French society was extremely simple. Unless one wishes to place the members of the clergy in a separate classification, there were only two social classes—nobles and serfs. Under these circumstances the integrity and exclusiveness of the feudal caste was secure, for it was practically impossible for a serf to rise high enough to knock at the doors of the aristocracy. The only route by which a serf might rise to high position was through the church, and as churchmen left no heirs, the fortunate few who succeeded were no menace to the feudal class. But in the twelfth century the appearance of towns produced a new class, the townsmen who as freemen occupied a special category between the nobles and the unfree rural laborers. Freedom alone would not have made them a serious menace to the exclusiveness of the aristocracy— the freeing of serfs during the twelfth and thirteenth centuries created a class of rural freemen who rarely worried their social superiors. The strength of the townsman lay in the fact that he had a money income which through thrift could be turned into cash capital. Before long there were merchants and master craftsmen who could adorn their bodies and fill their stomachs on a more lavish scale than most knights could afford. This blow to noble pride probably lay at the bottom of the furious hatred the knight bore toward the townsman. In fact one purpose of mediaeval sumptuary legislation was to prevent the burgher from vying with the noble in richness of dress.

Extravagant display in food, dress, and standard of living was not the only ladder by which townsmen tried to climb toward the social position occupied by the nobles. As the feudal caste was an aristocracy of land-holders, great social prestige was attached to the posses-sion of the soil. Hence ambitious townsmen were continually and often successfully seeking to buy the fiefs of impecunious knights. Although feudal legisla-tion sternly forbade such transactions and restricted knightly rank to men whose fathers had enjoyed it, many townsmen did manage to acquire land held by knight service. A more direct route to equality with the nobles lay through the service of feudal princes. Kings could grant patents of nobility and often rewarded in this way their faithful servants. By one means or an-other a continuous trickle of townsmen made its way into the ranks of the aristocracy. But while this process was extremely irritating to the pride of the nobility, it had little real effect on the exclusiveness of the feudal class. The few townsmen who succeeded in acquiring noble status were easily and quickly assimilated into the aristocracy. The noble caste had been unable to close its ranks completely to outsiders, but it retained its social dominance.

The position of the noble class in the last years of the

COLORADO MOUNTAIN COLLEGE--LRC--WEST

fifteenth century formed a sad contrast with that which
it had enjoyed in the eleventh. The aristocracy of
France had been impoverished and shorn of most of its
political and military functions. Professional administrators drawn from the townsman class composed the
personnel of the royal and princely governments. The
noble could neither make war on his neighbors nor
conclude treaties with them. His lands and men were
taxed at the pleasure of the princes and their bureau-
crats. Although he still retained his rights of justice over
the inhabitants of his lands, he was usually obliged to
exercise them through professional agents under the
close supervision of royal officials. On the field of battle
the aristocracy saw the predominant place in contemporary tactics occupied by trains of artillery and masses of
mercenary infantry. If the noble wished a military
career, his opportunities were confined to service as an
officer or as a member of one of the élite cavalry regiments. The noble *gendarmes* were still the pride of the
French army, but they formed a fairly small proportion
of the entire military establishment. Only in the social
realm did the aristocracy hold its position. So successfully did the nobles capitalize the proud tradition of
their caste that they were able to overcome the richest
of merchant rivals. While kings and princes entrusted
the business of government to townsmen, they still
sought their companions among the nobles.

As early as the first half of the fifteenth century
courtly life at the seats of the Burgundian dukes pre-
saged the future of the nobility of France. There the
magnificent revenues drawn from the trade and industry
of the Low Countries supplied the means for a truly

princely mode of life. In the glittering courts of Philip the Good and Charles the Bold noblemen toyed gently with the traditional occupations of their class, war and politics, while they devoted most of their energies to entertaining and pleasing their mighty masters. Affection for chivalric tradition moved Philip the Good to found the order of the Golden Fleece and to hold the splendid " banquet of the Pheasant " to celebrate his intention of going on a crusade, but the crusade never started and the chief duty of the knights of the Golden Fleece was to hold impressive ceremonies. The complicated court ritual which was to occupy the attention of a fair part of the nobility of France for the next three centuries had its origins in the households of these Burgundian dukes. The knights of France were learning to be gentlemen. There were still farmer nobles and soldier nobles, but the future belonged to the courtiers.

II

FEUDAL CHIVALRY

MEN have always admired some qualities as virtues
and deplored others as faults. The nature of ideas of
this sort in any society is governed by various forces—
tradition, environment, and exposure to alien influences.
In two later chapters I shall discuss the ethical ideas
which outside groups, the clergy and the ladies, attempted to impose on the feudal warriors of France, but
here my concern is with those that grew out of their
cultural tradition and actual function in society. As
these ideas developed in the mind of the noble, the
miles or *chevalier*, and represented his conception of the
perfect knight, they have a peculiar right to be termed
chivalric. The fact that most of the qualities which this
ideal demanded were those which best fitted a nobleman
to perform his functions in the feudal system moves me
to call these same ideas feudal. Hence I have adopted
the term feudal chivalry to describe the set of ethical
conceptions to be discussed in this chapter. The ideal
knight of feudal chivalry was the lineal descendant of
the heroes of Germanic legend and the ancestor of the
modern gentleman. In both these capacities he is of
interest to the social historian as an important stage in
the history of masculine ethics.

The cultural tradition and the environment of the
eleventh-century noble combined to instill in him an

admiration for martial qualities. The Teutonic barbarian and the Frankish aristocrat had prized personal
bravery, physical strength, and skill in the use of arms.
As warfare was the chief occupation of the nobleman,
he was bound to value the traits which made a man an
effective soldier. Summed up under the term prowess,
the ability to beat the other man in battle, these qualities
became the fundamental chivalric virtues. The knight
who lacked prowess, who was not a competent warrior,
was of little use to his lord, the church, or a lady.
Prowess enabled the knight to fulfill his function in
society—without it he was an object of scorn to his contemporaries. " Be *preux* " was the usual admonition
given to a young man as he received the ceremonial blow
that made him a knight.[1] To call a nobleman a *preu-
dome*, a man of prowess, was to pay him the highest
compliment known to the Middle Ages. Not until the
knight began to turn into a courtier did this virtue lose
any of its importance. Christine de Pisan and Casti-
glione, who were deeply imbued with the ideas of the
Renaissance, did not consider prowess the chief of all
admirable qualities, but even they ranked it high among
the attributes required of a gentleman.[2]

The man of prowess was not, however, of much benefit to his contemporaries unless he could be relied on to
use his military capacities to fulfill his obligations to
others. The members of the ancient Germanic *comita-*

---

[1] Léon Gautier, *La chevalerie* (Paris, Victor Palmé, 1884), p. 285.
[2] Christine de Pisan, *Le livre des faits et bonnes meurs du sage roy.
Charles le quint* (ed. Michaud and Poujoulat, *Nouvelle collection des
mémoires relatifs à l'histoire de France*, I and II). Baldassare Castig-
lione, *The book of the courtier* (translated by Boby, *Everyman's
Library*).

tus, those of the Frankish *truste*, and the Carolingian *vassi dominici* were valued for their loyalty to the man to whom they had sworn fidelity. The disappearance of organized government with the collapse of the Carolingian empire made observance of personal obligations still more important. As feudal society was preserved from complete anarchy only by the mutual contracts between lords and vassals, it was essential that the noblemen observe these contracts faithfully. Hence loyalty, general trustworthiness, joined prowess to form the two basic chivalric virtues. But while the importance of loyalty as an abstract quality was recognized by every noble and every writer on chivalry, they did not all agree on its proper object. To the feudal world it meant observance of the mutual obligations which bound the members of the caste. The churchman on the other hand considered loyalty to the Christian faith and to the church more desirable than fidelity to temporal contracts. Finally the extreme exponents of courtly love made the observance of its customs the object of knightly loyalty. These differences do not, however, alter the fact that the knight was expected to be completely loyal to his obligations.

While the early Teutons undoubtedly placed most stress on a warrior's prowess and loyalty, they admired the open-handed giver. Early German literature abounds with accounts of rich and costly gifts and the honor they gained for him who made them. Thus tradition suggested that the eleventh-century noble should admire lavish generosity. This virtue was vastly elevated in general estimation under the influence of twelfth-century propaganda. The wandering minstrels who composed and circulated the epic tales of knightly deeds depended for their living on the generosity of their noble patrons. Naturally they extolled *largesse* to the skies and placed it among the chief chivalric virtues. Hugh de Méry in his *Tornoiement de l'Antechrist* expresses the situation most frankly "If *Largesse* dies, we will die of poverty and misery." [3] In an earlier passage the same writer goes so far as to make prowess a mere follower of *largesse*.[4] Perhaps his idea was similar to that of the eminently practical baron Philip de Novarre who states that generosity can hide most faults. A rich man who lacks prowess but is known for his generosity will find plenty of good knights who will fight for him in the hope of bounty.[5] Philip's conception of generosity was not, however, in full accord with that of its most enthusiastic admirers. His was a balanced, conservative view. "Every man should be generous according to his wealth and social position . . . not all acts that fools call generosity are really generous; for waste is not generosity. One should give reasonably . . . ." [6] The minstrels were inclined to consider such caution as Philip's niggardly. The biographer of William Marshal stated that *gentillesse* or nobility was reared in the house of *largesse* and expressed his admiration for Henry the young king whose lavish generosity kept him in a perpetual state of bankruptcy.[7] Many knights accepted the views of the

---

[3] Huon de Méry, *Le tornoiement de l'Antechrist* (ed. P. Tarbé, Reims, 1851), p. 72.

[4] *Ibid.*, p. 49.

[5] Philippe de Navarre [Novarre], *Les quatre ages de l'homme* (ed. Marcel de Fréville, *Société des anciens textes français*, Paris, 1888), p. 13.

[6] *Ibid.*, pp. 73-4.

[7] *L'histoire de Guillaume le Maréchal, comte de Striguil et de Pem-*

writers. Bertrand de Born had no use for the man who lived within his means. The true nobleman would mortgage his estates to gain funds for extending lavish hospitality and giving magnificent presents.[8] The persistent propaganda of hungry minstrels and impecunious knights raised *largesse* so high in the estimation of the feudal class that it was considered the primary characteristic of the noble. According to Stephen of Bourbon a great preacher was asked by a group of knights to name the chief noble virtue, and he proved to their complete satisfaction that the position belonged to *largesse*.[9] Although throughout the Middle Ages there were sensible writers who limited the exercise of this virtue as did Philip de Novarre, chivalric generosity tended to become more and more closely identified with reckless extravagance. Long after prowess and loyalty had lost their peculiar applicability to men of high birth, a complete disregard of caution in the use of money was considered the mark of a nobleman.

The seeds at least of the knightly ideals of prowess, loyalty, and generosity existed in the cultural tradition of the noble class and needed only the nourishment provided by twelfth-century France to spring into full flower, but another chivalric ideal, courtesy, seems to have grown directly out of the feudal environment. Now courtesy as used by mediaeval writers had a wide variety of meanings. In so far as it referred to the ability of a knight to please the ladies, it was the product

---

broke (ed. Paul Meyer, *Société de l'histoire de France*, Paris, 1891-1901), I, lines 5065-5094.

[8] Joseph Anglade, *Anthologie des troubadours* (Paris, n. d.), p. 61.

[9] *Anecdotes historiques d'Etienne de Bourbon* (ed. A. Lecoy de la Marche, *Société de l'histoire de France*, Paris, 1877), pp. 245-6.

of the romantic influence and will be discussed in a later chapter. Here our interest must be confined to courtesy as applied to the relations between noblemen. As the heritability of fiefs became firmly established in the tenth and eleventh centuries it led to the stabilization of the feudal class and to the development of class consciousness. In time the idea appeared that nobles deserved special consideration from their fellows. One result of this feeling was the growth of interest in courtesy in its narrowest sense, ordinary politeness in conversation and social relations. All chivalric writers agree that a good knight should be polite to his fellows. [10] But the class consciousness of the nobles showed itself in more practical forms of courtesy. By the twelfth century feudal opinion seems to have required that the hardships of war should be ameliorated through mutual consideration shown to noble by noble. This tendency appears in some of the cruder *chansons de geste.* When Gaydon had cut off the head of his opponent in a duel, he laid two swords crosswise on his foe's body. This moved the Emperor Charles to cry " Ha! God, how courteous this duke is! " [11] In *Raoul de Cambrai* Bernier had by devious stratagems persuaded his enemy to step naked into a fountain while he himself stood by armed, yet he refused to kill the helpless man. Such a deed would cause him to be an object of scorn and reproach all his days.[12] This belief that it was unethical to attack

[10] See for instance Philippe de Navarre, *Les quatre ages de l'homme,* p. 13.

[11] *Gaydon* (ed. F. Guessard and S. Luce, *Les anciens poetes de la France,* Paris, 1862), pp. 55-6.

[12] *Raoul de Cambrai* (ed. P. Meyer and A. Longnon, *Société des anciens textes française,* Paris, 1882), p. 256.

an unarmed man is illustrated throughout the *chansons
de geste* and is one of the few courteous principles
mentioned in this literature. The Arthurian works of
Chrétien de Troyes show these ideas in a more developed form. When the hero of a tale overthrows a
villainous knight, he practically always spares his life
and releases him on parole. No one attacks an unarmed
man. Two knights never set upon one. Even bands of
robbers who meet an adventuring knight are careful to
assault him one by one. While this picture of the most
wicked knights scrupulously observing the requirements
of courtesy may be regarded as rather fanciful, there
seems little doubt that feudal propriety demanded that
knights fight each other on essentially equal terms and
that the vanquished be treated with consideration. In
Froissart's opinion a true knight would show every
possible courtesy to his noble prisoners, would quickly
release them on parole, and would set their ransoms at
sums easily within their means.[13] All this was merely
the courtesy one knight owed to another.

   In addition to developing the chivalric conceptions of
prowess, loyalty, generosity, and courtesy the knights of
twelfth-century France produced an ethical rationali-
zation which seemed to endow their endless turbulence
and violence with an elevated motive. Prestige has
always been dear to man, and in warlike societies it is
usually based on fame for soldierly deeds. The broader
conception of glory that would be perpetuated through
future generations has been equally common. The early
German warrior liked to think that his prowess would

---

[13] *Chroniques de J. Froissart* (ed. Siméon Luce, *Société de l'histoire
de France*, Paris, 1869-1878), V, 64-5.

long be the subject for song and story just as the Roman legate dreamed of a triumphal arch to celebrate his victories. Affection for prestige and desire for glory were part of the inheritance of the mediaeval nobleman. But in the early feudal period the bitterness of the struggle for survival forced these ideas to play a minor rôle. The eleventh-century knight fought for the means of subsis-tence—land, plunder, ransoms. This view of the purpose of war was neatly expressed by Bertrand de Born in a poem written in joyful anticipation of a conflict between Richard the Lionhearted and Alphonse of Castille.

And it will be good to live for one will take the property of usurers and there will no longer be a peaceful pack-horse on the roads, all the townsmen will tremble; the merchant will no longer journey in peace on the road to France. He who wishes to enrich himself will only need to steal well.[14]

Bertrand was a man of no reticence. While undoubtedly many of his contemporaries shared his reasons for loving war, few would have avowed them so frankly. By his day, the latter part of the twelfth century, various cir-cumstances had combined to encourage knights to claim a more lofty motive for their fighting. As war became more and more a contest between feudal princes rather than between local lords, the knight found it more difficult to believe that he fought to protect his fief and its inhabitants. The gradual replacement of the feudal levy by paid knights weakened the idea that one went to war to serve one's lord. The knight was left with profit, pay, booty, ransoms, as his sole motive. Since the

---

[14] Anglade, *Anthologie des troubadours*, pp. 65-6.

church frowned particularly on fighting for profit, he
was inclined to seek another purpose. Then too as wars
grew less frequent the knights turned their energies
to tourneying, but few liked to admit that they entered
these chivalric sports for profit. Thus there was a clear
need for a noble reason for following their traditional
occupation, and one was easily found. The knight of
the twelfth century passed the long evenings listening
to tales of the great heroes of the past. Naturally it
occurred to him that it would be pleasant to have his
own deeds recounted long after his death. From this
idea grew the conception that glory was the true aim of
a good knight. He would, in theory at least, practice the
chivalric virtues for reputation—to be known through
the ages as a perfect knight. This idea that the desire
for glory was the proper motive for a knight can be seen
very clearly in the *Histoire de Guillaume le Maréchal*.[15]
Again and again the author asserts that William had no
interest in capturing horses, arms, or noble prisoners.
His sole purpose was to acquire glory. Philip de Novarre
in his usual practical manner combines glory with profit
as the aims of a knight. "The young nobleman, the
knight, and other men-at-arms should work to acquire
honor so as to be renowned for valor and to gain temporal goods, riches, and inheritances."[16] In another passage in which he discusses the advantages of chivalry
as a career Philip points out that many knights have
been honored by having their deeds recorded in stories,
poems, and epics.[17] By Froissart's time the profit motive

[15] *Histoire de Guillaume le Maréchal.* See also Sidney Painter,
William Marshal (Baltimore, 1933).
[16] Philippe de Navarre, *Les quatre ages de l'homme*, p. 39.
[17] *Ibid.*, p. 12.

as a reason for fighting had lost all its respectability. Knights fought to win glory, and the function of the historian was to see that no worthy deed went unrecorded and that the honor was distributed fairly.[18]

Having discussed the various chivalric ideals which were developed by the feudal class under the influence of its tradition and environment, we must now examine these ideas in practice. We must discover if possible to what extent the nobles of France were actually competent warriors, loyal, generous, courteous, and avid for glory. As the knight was primarily a soldier and a vassal, prowess and loyalty were the basic qualities which he had to possess if he were to fulfill his functions in society. A full discussion of the knight as soldier and vassal would obviously involve the entire military and political history of mediaeval France. All that can be done here is to supply a few broad and rather tentative generalizations. By the end of the twelfth century the knights of France were noted throughout the world for their prowess in battle. The biographer of William Marshal considered them definitely superior to their close relatives who formed the chivalry of England.[19] A contemporary of William's, Giraldus Cambrensis, believed that in military glory the knights of France surpassed those of all other nations.[20] The French played so dominant a part in the crusades both in Spain and in Palestine that the Moslems called all crusaders Franks. Norman knights supported by those of neighboring

[18] *Chroniques de Froissart*, I, 1-2.

[19] *Histoire de Guillaume le Maréchal*, I, lines 4481-4484; II, lines 16388-16391.

[20] Giraldus Cambrensis, *De principis instructione liber* (ed. G. F. Warner in *Giraldi Cambrensis opera, VIII, Rolls Series*), p. 318.

provinces conquered England, Ireland, lowland Scot-
land, Sicily, and southern Italy. In general it can be
said that during the twelfth and thirteenth century the
French knights met no troops except the Turks who
could stand up against them in battle. While they suffered several severe defeats at the hands of Turkish
armies, disasters like Tiberias and Mansourah were
more the result of faulty leadership than of any lack of
prowess on the part of the knights. Moreover such
brilliant victories as Bouvines and Muret gained against
European enemies had far more influence on the prestige of the knights of France than their failures in the
distant lands of Palestine and Egypt. The first great
blow to the reputation of the French came in 1302
when the feudal levy of the kingdom was routed at
Courtrai by the Flemish townsmen, but here again the
defeat was caused by the ineptness of the French commanders. Not until Duke Philip of Orleans and his
division fled without striking a blow from the field of
Poitiers did serious doubts arise in France about the
fighting ability of its noble knights. In short Turkish
light horse, Flemish townsmen, and English bowmen
when given their choice of position could defeat French
knights, but none of these troops could face them successfully on ground suited to the heavy feudal cavalry.
If knightly prowess had been mental as well as physical,
if the tactical ability of the noble leaders had equalled
the courage and skill in the use of arms shown by their
knights, the chivalry of France need not have suffered
these blows to its prestige. Despite such isolated incidents as the flight of Orleans at Poitiers it can be said
that the knights of France retained throughout the

Middle Ages the courage, hardiness, and skill in arms that won them fame in the twelfth and thirteenth centuries. In fact they may have increased in pure physical strength. To bear and use the frightfully heavy equipment of a fifteenth-century knight must have required remarkable dexterity and stamina. We are assured that Marshal Boucicaut as a young man could turn a somersault fully armed except for his helmet and when completely equipped for battle could vault on a horse or climb the under side of a scaling ladder using his hands alone.[21] While it is perfectly possible that the good Marshal may have boasted a bit to his earnest biographer, the fact that such feats were considered within the realm of possibility is a decided tribute to the prowess of fifteenth-century knights.

Although reasonably satisfactory generalizations about the prowess of mediaeval French knights can be based on its obvious results, the winning or losing of battles, no such course is open with respect to loyalty. Any statement about the practice of this latter quality must be founded purely on the impression left on one's mind by a large number of individual incidents and hence can be nothing more than the expression of a personal opinion. With this reservation I venture to make the generalization that a nobleman rarely violated his feudal obligations as they were interpreted by his class. The limitation expressed in the last clause is obviously of primary importance. Historians have described the feudal aristocrat as habitually perfidious, and even when

[21] *Le livre des faicts du bon Messire Jean le Maingre, dit Boucicaut* (ed. Michaud and Poujoulat, *Nouvelle collection des mémoires relatifs à l'histoire de France*, II, Paris, 1881), pp. 219-220.

the historian makes no moral judgment modern readers
have drawn that conclusion from his account of the
behavior of the nobles. We are inclined to examine
the feudal oath and contemporary customary law, interpret them according to our own ideas, and condemn acts
which seem to us to violate the feudal contract. While
this mode of thought is natural, from the point of view
of historical methodology it is utterly fantastic. Ethical
principles are established by contemporary opinion, not
by law. We are little troubled when a friend is convicted
of speeding, but we would be profoundly shocked were
he found guilty of forgery. Yet if a future generation
should take the former offense more seriously, it would
be possible for a historian to describe the sons of Presi-
dent Roosevelt as habitual criminals on the ground that
they were frequently arrested for violating the speed
laws. In short we interpret our laws as freely as the
feudal noble interpreted his customary law. The noble
class of mediaeval France had well established standards
of loyalty to feudal obligations. When King Philip
Augustus exacted promises from a vassal, he knew pretty
closely what performance he could count on. Let me
take an example from the turbulent career of Peter of
Dreux, duke of Brittany. From our point of view he
continually violated his general feudal obligations and
his solemn oaths, but this was clearly not the opinion
of his contemporaries. Apparently only once did he
cross the line set by his class. When he made an alliance
with the king of England after specifically swearing
that he would not do so, his fellow barons assembled in

King Louis' court solemnly condemned him.[22] In general the feudal class scorned the noble who did not maintain its standards of loyalty. William Marshal reproved King Philip Augustus for taking advantage of the treasonable behavior of several of King John's Norman castellans.[23] Froissart was unable to believe that as good a knight as Oliver de Cliçon was capable of treason " But I think it most unlikely that so noble and so gentle a knight and so powerful a man could think of and arrange falseness or treason." [24] In short I believe that most nobles observed their feudal obligations to the extent that the common opinion of their class required.

When the feudal bond was not involved, knightly loyalty appears in an even better light. Violation of parole or of a solemn promise was exceedingly rare. Writing in the twelfth century Orderic Vitalis quotes William Rufus as saying " Far from me would it be to believe that an honest knight would violate his parole. If he did, he would be forever an object of contempt as a man outside the law." [25]

The sceptical and far from chivalrously inclined King John considered that to require his disaffected barons to make charters promising to be faithful to him was an effective means of preventing a revolt, and very few barons appeared in arms against him until those charters had been formally invalidated by *Magna Carta*. Frois-

---

[22] Sidney Painter, *The scourge of the clergy, Peter of Dreux, duke of Brittany* (Baltimore, 1937).

[23] *Histoire de Guillaume le Maréchal*, II, lines 12687-12700. Painter, *William Marshal*, p. 134.

[24] *Chroniques de Froissart*, III, 35.

[25] Orderici Vitalis, *Historiae ecclesiasticae* (ed. August le Prevost, Société de l'histoire de France, Paris, 1838-1855), IV, 49.

sart and his contemporaries assumed that a knight's word was good, and they furnish examples of rather amazing promises faithfully observed. For instance on one occasion John, duke of Normandy, the future King John the Good of France, lay with his host at St. Quentin preparing to raid the duchy of Hainault. One night the seneschal of Hainault with a few followers slipped into St. Quentin and captured a French noble. The prisoner gave his word to meet the seneschal at Valenciennes, the capital of Hainault, three days later, and the seneschal retired from the town with full and justified confidence that his captive would appear on the appointed day.[26] King John of France, who had been captured at Poitiers, was released from his English prison in exchange for a number of hostages. When one of these hostages was so unchivalrous as to escape, the king returned to prison in London. In short there is plenty of evidence to show that as a rule the knights of France were most scrupulous in keeping their plighted word.

The practice of generosity requires no extended discussion. It was woven deeply into the fabric of noble life in mediaeval France. On the field of battle or in the council chamber a knight might be esteemed according to his prowess or loyalty, but elsewhere his worth was judged by the lavishness of his hospitality and the magnificence of his gifts. The *Histoire de Guillaume le Maréchal* contains a pleasant little example of knightly *largesse*. One day William was waiting fully armed for a tournament to begin. Just as the first knight of the opposing side came into view, a young herald asked William for a gift. Leaping on his horse

---

[26] *Chroniques de Froissart*, II, 10-11.

the Marshal rode at the other knight, overthrew him, and presented the mount of the vanquished to the herald.[27] This combination of prowess and generosity was greatly admired as a chivalric exploit. The practice of knightly generosity on a grand scale can be seen in the register of the Black Prince, eldest son of King Edward III of England. A few entries must suffice as examples.

> A gold mug, made like a wine cask; to the lord of Castelnau of Burgundy when he ate with the prince at Caleis.
>
> A small gold mug; to the lady Isabel de Trokesford when she ate with the prince at the same place.
>
> A destrier called Morel de Burgherssh; to a minstrel at a tournament at Bury St. Edmunds, 22 Edward III.
>
> A pony called Dun Crump; to a knight of Almain at Caleis.
>
> Two dozen hoods for falcons . . . ; to divers knights and squires of the prince's household.
>
> Two pairs of spurs, . . . ; to the lord of Tankevill and his brother.
>
> . . . a silver cup, weighing 78s 3d and bought at twice that amount, together with £13 6s 8d placed therein, given by the prince to the lady Eleanor Giffard.
>
> . . . a cup, silver-gilt, weighing £4 3s 4d and bought at twice that amount, given by the prince to the wife of Adam Louches. . . .[28]

As few knights could afford to be as lavish as the Black Prince, his case cannot be called typical, but it shows how *largesse* was practiced by one whom his contemporaries admired as a paragon of chivalry.

[27] *Histoire de Guillaume le Maréchal*, I, lines 3489-3520. Painter, *William Marshal*, p. 41.

[28] *Register of Edward the Black Prince* (Rolls Series), IV, 66-77, 89. There are many similar accounts in the four volumes.

The last two ideals of feudal chivalry, courtesy and love of glory, may be treated together. Although both could be practiced in peaceful surroundings, they can be illustrated most strikingly by martial incidents. The chronicles tell little of ordinary politeness between nobles, but they are filled with accounts of courtesies exchanged by combatants. While a knight might hope that loyalty and generosity would heighten his reputation, it was to prowess on the field of battle that he looked for true fame. Of course any discussion of whether or not knights really fought for glory is utterly futile. One cannot delve into the mind of a man long dead and discern his motive. I can simply present examples that seem to me to represent battle primarily for glory—cases in which I can think of no other reasonable motive. Hence the next few paragraphs will consist of a study of the process by which courtesy ameliorated the hardships of war and a few examples of men who fought for no discernible motive except glory.

The earliest instances of knightly courtesy in the realm of war appeared in the late eleventh and early twelfth centuries. Orderic Vitalis praised William Rufus for his treatment of knights. He never held noble prisoners in chains, but released them on parole.[29] A generation later the biographer of Count Geoffrey of Anjou gives an illuminating incident. While sitting at table one day Geoffrey saw some knightly prisoners who were fettered, unkempt, and garbed in dirty, torn clothes. " If we are knights, we ought to pity knights. Free them from chains, bathe them and cut their hair, give them

---

[29] Orderic Vitalis, IV, 44, 49.

new clothes, and let them sit with me at table." [30]
Another pleasant tale of knightly courtesy is told by
Walter Map. Louis VI of France was at war with Count
Thibaut of Blois and Chartres and one day he planned
an ambush for his enemy. After secreting himself with
a strong force near Chartres, he sent a small party up
to the walls in the hope that the count would sorty from
the town and be led into the ambush. Just as everything was ready, Count Thibaut, unprepared and slen-
derly escorted, rode past the ambush. King Louis absolutely refused to allow his men to attack. He would have
been glad to have captured Thibaut by a clever stratagem, but he declined to take advantage of pure chance.
Hence the king simply sent word to Thibaut that he
should ride about less casually in time of war and returned to Paris with his troops. [31] Examples of this sort
could be multiplied, but not to any great extent. The
twelfth century saw courtesy on battle fields and kindly
treatment of noble captives, but it also saw knights
passing their lives in grim prisons and others savagely
mutilated. War was still a serious business, and courtesy
could only slowly ameliorate its savagery. In fact the
courteous practices that were to make war a pleasant
sport as far as the nobles were concerned seem to have
developed less on the field of battle than on the tourney
ground.

The origins of the tournament are lost in the obscurity
that shrouds most phases of the history of the early

[30] *Historia Gaufredi ducis Normannorum et comitis Andegavorum*
(ed. Louis Halphen and René Poupardin, *Chroniques des comtes
d'Anjou et des seigneurs d'Amboise*, Paris, 1913), pp. 195-6.
[31] Walter Map, *De nugis curialium* (translated by Montague R.
James, *Cymmrodorion record series*, London, 1923), p. 252.

Middle Ages. It has been suggested that the tourney was the lineal descendant of the rough martial games of the early Germans, but the evidence of continuity which would give this theory historical validity is entirely lacking.[32] One can merely say that tournaments began to be mentioned in the eleventh century and were common by the middle of the twelfth.[33] It is not, however, difficult to produce a plausible explanation for their appearance. As war was the chief occupation and interest of the nobleman, he probably always spent much of his spare time in military exercises. Tilting at a ring was a well recognized manner of demonstrating skill with horse and lance. It seems equally likely that knights would ride at each other in sport while exercising in the castle yard. But in the tenth and early eleventh centuries there was no reason for an extensive development of martial sports. The knights obtained their amusement and exercise in arms in the continuous warfare that marked the period. It was only when the rising feudal princes began to check private war that knights began to find time lying heavy on their hands. By the twelfth century wars were fought when called for by the policy of great lords rather than when knights grew bored. As a result the nobles found themselves faced with long, dull periods of peace. Perhaps even more serious for the poorer knights was the fact that peace meant no income from booty and ransoms. Under these conditions it was only natural that it should occur to someone that martial sports and exercise would be both more exciting and more profitable if they took the form of

[32] Gautier, La chevalerie, p. 675.
[33] Ibid., pp. 675-6.

regular pitched battles arranged in advance. Be that as
it may, by the latter part of the twelfth century the
tournament was a flourishing institution in northern
France. The author of the *Histoire de Guillaume le
Maréchal* asserts that there was a tourney held some-
where in the region every fortnight.[34] The same source
shows clearly the reasons for these meetings, both real
and avowed. Knights needed exercise in the use of
arms and opportunities to acquire glory. Less strongly
emphasized but no less definitely expressed was the
boredom with peace and desire for ransoms. While one
is inclined to doubt the reality of the knights' consuming
desire to improve their skill in the use of arms, it seems
very likely that the numerous tourneys held in France
contributed something to the prowess of French knights.
Effective use of knightly arms demanded continual practice, and this the tournament provided. But whatever
may have been the value of the tourney as a school
for soldiers, it was an invaluable breeding ground for
chivalric practices.

The tournaments of the twelfth century differed but
little from ordinary battles. When a prolonged period
of peace, say six months or more, made life grow dull
and knights feel rusty, some rich and chivalrously inclined feudal prince would decide to hold a tourney.
He would select as a site a pleasant meadow in his lands
and then send heralds about the countryside to announce
the affair. For instance the count of Dreux might des-
patch his heralds to proclaim that on a certain day the
knights of Normandy would combat those of France
between the villages of Anet and Sorel-Moussel in the

---

[34] *Histoire de Guillaume le Maréchal*, I, lines 4974-5.

valley of the Eure. On the appointed day the knights
would gather on the field, put on their armor in safety-
zones provided for the purpose, and line up in opposing
ranks. Then when a herald gave the signal the two
lines of heavy feudal cavalry would level their lances
and charge full tilt. Once the lances were broken, the
knights would draw their swords and continue the contest. There were no restrictions on the number of
knights on either side and when one party was bested
and sought to retire, the victors harried them through
the countryside in the hope of capturing as many as
possible. Occasionally one party would conceal an infantry force to cover its retreat. That flower of chivalrous princes, Philip of Alsace, count of Flanders, was
not above bringing into the tournament itself infantry-
men armed with hooks for dragging knights from their
horses. The monk of Montaudon suggests that some
nobles went so far as to use crossbowmen in tourneys.[35]
These practices were frowned on—the tournament was
a knightly affair and infantry had no place in it. There
was, however, another device used by the count of Flanders that was apparently acceptable. He and his men
would arm and announce that they were going to watch
the tourney. Then when the contestants grew tired, the
count would enter the field and capture large numbers
of his exhausted opponents. In short as long as only
knights took part, any stratagem was in order. There
were two respects in which these combats differed from
regular battles. Places of refuge were provided where
the knights could put on their armor in preparation for
the tourney and to which they could retire if they suff-

---

[35] André Berry, *Florilège des troubadours* (Paris, 1930), p. 361.

ered some such disaster as having the laces of a helmet broken. Moreover when a knight was overcome and surrendered to his opponent, he was released at once on parole. After the tournament the knights who had been captured sought out their conquerors to arrange for ransom. Apparently in most cases the penalty for the defeated was limited to the loss of horse and armor, and this equipment was usually redeemed by a cash payment. Thus the provision of safety-zones and re-strictions on the financial losses that were possible were the only differences between tournaments and regular battles.[36]

Despite its close resemblance to the savage melée of feudal warfare, the twelfth-century tournament was a fertile breeding ground for the courteous practices of chivalry. After the contest the richer knights held open house for friend and foe in their quarters. Often indeed the lord who sponsored the tourney would give a great feast for the participants. These social activities tended to increase the feeling of friendliness among the con-testants and remove the tournament further from the animosities of war. Then as the courtly idea that the true purpose of glory won by prowess was to gain the affection and esteem of a lady developed, women began to play a more prominent part in tournaments. A group of ladies watched one of the contests in which William Marshal took part, and his biographer assures us that their bright eyes moved him to outdo himself in valor. On another occasion a great lady, probably Marie, coun-

---

[36] The most extensive source of information about twelfth-century tournaments is the *Histoire de Guillaume le Maréchal*. See Painter, *William Marshal*, pp. 23-60, especially pp. 56-59.

tess of Champagne, presented William with a prize to reward him for his prowess.[37] Soon a gallery of ladies was an essential part of every well-ordered tournament. These various influences were bound to lessen the savagery of these contests. Bit by bit as time went on the tournament became a festival instead of a mere substitute for warfare. The first step in the amelioration of the ferocity of martial sports came with the development of the joust or single combat between two knights. Although jousts are referred to by twelfth-century writers, the fact that they are barely mentioned in the *Histoire de Guillaume le Maréchal* indicates that they were not yet a popular form of knightly sport. Nevertheless certain incidents in the *Histoire* suggest that when knights arrived on the field early they were inclined to amuse themselves by fighting single combats while waiting for the melée to begin. Certainly by the middle of the thirteenth century most tournaments were preceded by a series of jousts. The joust was far milder and less dangerous than the wild melée and therefore it grew in favor at the expense of the other. The general combats became more and more rare until many affairs that were called tournaments were in reality merely a series of jousts. Then during the same period, the thirteenth and fourteenth centuries, it began to be customary to use special blunted weapons in tourney and joust. With these changes went the development of complicated rules and regulations that turned martial sports into comparatively gentle games.

The tournaments of the fifteenth century were pri-

[37] *Histoire de Guillaume le Maréchal*, I, lines 3041-3148, 3455-3552. Painter, *William Marshal*, pp. 40-41.

marily festivals and pageants rather than trials of prowess. They lasted several days, and the major part of the time was occupied with feasts and dances. On the rare occasions when a melée was part of the affair, it consisted simply of two parties charging each other and breaking their blunted and intentionally fragile lances. The fierce general combats with the sword were things of the past. The jousts which were the chief feature of most festivities of this sort were like modern prize fights. The contestants rode at each other a set number of times. If one was unhorsed in accordance with the rules, it was a knockout. Usually, however, neither won decisively and the decision was given on points. For instance to lose a stirrup meant defeat in that tilt. Sometimes the jousts included combats on foot, but these were also strictly regulated. Each contestant was allowed a certain number of strokes with sword or battle-ax, and here again the victory was usually decided on points as the massive armor of the period made it essentially improbable that either participant would be hurt. In fact so heavy and cumbersome was the knightly equipment that a contestant who fell down was practically out of the combat.

One of the most interesting features of the martial sports of the latter part of the fourteenth and fifteenth centuries was the series of jousts arranged by individuals. During the lull in the Hundred Years War that marked the last years of the fourteenth century Marshal Boucicaut found himself at a loss to think of ways of acquiring glory. Finally he " planned an enterprise the most high, most gracious, and most honorable that any Christian knight had undertaken for a long time." He and two

companions would take up their residence for a month
on the frontier between the county of Boulogne and the
English town of Calais. Three months in advance
heralds would go through England, Aragon, Germany,
and Italy announcing the Marshal's intention to be at
the appointed place from March 20 to April 20. Each of
the three knights would be ready to meet all challengers
on any day except Friday. Enemies of France could
choose whether they were to contend with real lances
or with blunted tilting weapons. Friends of the Marshal's country would be met with blunted lances. Each
contest was to consist of five tilts. When the appointed
time had come, Boucicaut set up four magnificent
pavilions on a lovely meadow, three for himself and his
companions and one for their opponents. He also laid
in a vast supply of food and wine so that he could
lavishly entertain his large escort of knights, squires,
heralds, trumpeters, and minstrels and also offer sump-
tuous hospitality to knights who came to fight. In front
of the tents of Boucicaut and his companions stood a
great oak. On each of three branches hung two shields,
one for friends and one for foes, and a supply of pointed
and blunt lances, while another branch was adorned
with a horn. Under each pair of shields was the coat-
of-arms of the knight to whom it belonged. When a
knight appeared who desired to joust, he would blow
the horn and strike one of the shields. Thus if he were
an Englishman who wished to tilt with Boucicaut he
would strike the shield of the Marshal which was re-
served for foes of the realm of France. According to the
Marshal's biographer the affair was a great success.
During the month the three companions jousted against

one hundred and twenty English knights and forty from other lands. Their English opponents included such distinguished figures as Henry of Lancaster, earl of Derby, later King Henry IV, and John of Holland, earl of Huntingdon. We are assured that although the three knights wounded many challengers, they themselves suffered no injuries.

This "noble enterprise" of the Marshal Boucicaut may be taken as typical of many similar affairs.[38] Some years later Jacques de Lalaing, a noble Burgundian knight, held a series of jousts with even more entrancing arrangements. For one thing a beautiful lady replaced the oak tree as a post on which to hang the defender's shields. Prospective challengers were expected to prove that they were sprung from four noble lines to the satisfaction of a herald who accompanied the shield-bearing lady. The lady carried three shields, white, violet, and black. A challenger who struck the white shield could exchange as many blows of the ax as he chose with Lalaing. The violet shield meant a similar contest with swords, while he who struck the black shield was committed to twenty-five tilts with the lance. A sad comment on the chivalry of the day is the provision that in the combats on horseback neither contestant should be tied to his saddle. The penalties provided for the losers were fantastic. For instance if a knight were knocked down in the combat with axes he was obliged to wear a gold bracelet for a year unless before that he could find the lady who held the key. The knight who had his ax struck from his hand was to offer a diamond to the most beautiful lady of France.

[38] *Livre des faicts du Maréchal de Boucicaut*, pp. 230-232.

Every challenger was to receive a wand the color of the shield he struck as a memento of the occasion. As William Marshal turns violently in his grave, let us leave the fifteenth-century joust.[39]

During the fourteenth century the courteous practices which had developed in the tournament were applied on the field of battle. The knights of the twelfth century had conducted their martial games like battles—their descendants made their battles resemble tourneys. The nobles who fought under the banners of France and England in the Hundred Years War had little direct personal interest in the result. National patriotism had not yet appeared as an important force and devotion to a liege lord was rarely strong enough to move a knight to make sacrifices for his suzerain. The nobles fought because war was their traditional occupation and because they were paid to. As a result the desire for glory became the avowed and in the case of many individuals the real motive for military activities. Glory was the chief object in both battle and tourney and it could be won as much by courtesy as by prowess. The pleasant kindnesses and social amenities of the joust and tournament were carried over into the conduct of war—often to the decided detriment of military effectiveness. War became a martial sport. This attitude is clearly indicated in contemporary chronicles. In 1304 according to the *Chronique Normande* the chivalrous entourage of King Philip V urged him to make peace with the Flemings. They were a cruel people who made war mortally with-

---

[39] *Livre des faits de Jacques de Lalaing* (ed. Kervyn de Lettenhove, *Oeuvres de Georges Chastellain*, VIII, Bruxelles, 1866), pp. 188-197.

out ransom.[40] Froissart remarks about the duke of Hainault who bent all his energies to preserving his duchy from a French invasion that " he took this war too much to heart." [41]

What this spirit meant in the actual conduct of military operations can best be shown by a few examples. On one occasion the duke of Lancaster was invading Champagne from the north and the duke of Bourbon was watching the region from Troyes. The captain of the garrison at Plancy, a minor fortress on Lancaster's path, notified the duke of Bourbon that the English were about to pass near his stronghold. If the duke would send him fifty good men, they could have a " *belle adventure.*" Bourbon immediately despatched fifty picked knights and squires. When these gay nobles arrived at Plancy, they built a barrier just outside its main gate and named it " *La Barrière Amoureuse.*" Then as soon as the English appeared they sallied out, got behind their barrier, and challenged the English knights to combat. A fair number of the latter, as thirsty for glory as their opponents, dismounted and attacked the barrier.[42] The result was a gentlemanly fight that reflected glory on everyone and was of no military value. The duke of Lancaster had no intention of assaulting Plancy, and the troops in the fortress were too few to be any danger to him. It was simply a pleasant passage at arms.

A still more illuminating incident comes from the

[40] *Chronique Normande du XIVe siècle* (ed. A. and E. Molinier, Société de l'histoire de France, Paris, 1882), p. 27.

[41] *Chroniques de Froissart,* II, 69.

[42] *La chronique du bon duc Loys de Bourbon* (ed. A. Chazaud, Société de l'histoire de France, Paris, 1876), pp. 50-52.

career of this same duke of Bourbon. The duke had invested the castle of Verteuil in Poitou. The castellan, Bartholomew de Montprivat, was absent, but he had left the fortress in charge of a noble squire named Regnaud de Montferrand. The place was so strong and the defense so effective that Bourbon soon decided that it could be taken only by mining. After about a month of hard labor the mine was completed so that it afforded a passage into the interior of the castle. When the duke learned of its completion, it occurred to him that here was a chance for a fine chivalrous passage at arms. He sent his lieutenant up to the castle gate to inquire whether there was any knight inside who would like to meet another knight in the mine. The garrison replied that they could not boast a knight but that a noble gentleman would be glad to accept the challenge. Bourbon then armed and descended into the mine while Regnaud came to meet him from the other side. There in the narrow passage, it was only eighteen inches wide, the two men fought with their swords. Despite the fact that it could hardly have been more than a poking match which could not have been dangerous for men in full armor, Bourbon grew very excited and gave his war cry. Immediately his opponent asked if he were indeed Duke Louis of Bourbon. The dignity of his foe overwhelmed Regnaud. "I praise God that he has today done me the grace and honor to fight so valiant a prince." After expressing this pious sentiment he cooly offered to surrender the castle if the duke would dub him knight. Bourbon, who was not too much of a gentleman to be cautious, demanded the keys in advance. Regnaud immediately surrendered the keys and was duly knighted.

The two commanders then agreed that it would be selfish of them to have the castle surrender at once and thus prevent their men from enjoying the mine. Hence the surrender was planned for the next day. Meanwhile the gentlemen of both sides could disport themselves in the mine. The next morning the garrison rode out of the castle. Bourbon gave Regnaud a horse and a belt and they exchanged courteous compliments. Thus a nobleman was so appreciative of the glory gained from fighting the duke of Bourbon and of the honor of being knighted by him that he surrendered an important castle entrusted to his care. The chronicler assures us that everyone who heard of this affair was filled with admiration for the courtesy of the two participants.[43] One would like, however, to have the comments of the absent castellan of Verteuil and his superior, the English seneschal of Guienne.

The absorbing interest in gaining glory through the practice of prowess and courtesy to the almost complete exclusion of any consideration for practical military objectives is best illustrated in the pages of Froissart. This chronicler frankly states in his prologue that he is writing so that " the great marvels and beautiful feats of arms may be notably registered." [44] In fact he uses this purpose as a basis for assigning to various sorts of men their proper function in society. The warriors strive to win glory, the common people talk about their deeds, and the clergy write down their feats of arms.[45] To Froissart the Hundred Years War was a long series of

---

[43] *Chronique de Loys de Bourbon*, pp. 149-152.
[44] *Chroniques de Froissart*, I, 1.
[45] *Ibid.*, p. 5.

knightly deeds. He had little interest in the fundamental tactics of battles and sieges, but turned his attention to the "beautiful skirmishes" where small groups
of knights demonstrated their prowess. The interminable siege of Hennebont which was marked by few
bloody assaults but by many small affrays between the
garrison and its foes delighted him. Then he described
with relish the numerous arranged combats between
equal parties of knights. It was not unusual to settle
such questions as the possession of a castle by an affair
of this sort. Froissart was particularly fond of recounting
the courteous treatment accorded to one another by
noble foes. He praised the English not for the military
skill that won them battle after battle, but for their
kindness to their prisoners and the reasonableness of the
ransoms they demanded.[46] Edward III informed Hervey
de Léon, a great Breton noble who had been captured
by the English, that he well knew he could pay easily
a ransom of forty thousand *écus*, but he would release
him for ten thousand if he would be kind enough to
bear the king's defiance to King Philip of France.[47]
Still more illuminating is Froissart's account of a conversation between the Black Prince and the Constable
Bertrand du Quesclin who had fallen into the hands of
the English while aiding King Henry of Castille. One
morning the prince asked Bertrand how he was. The
constable replied " Thank God, I was never better and
it is right I should be well for I am the most honored
knight of the world since I remain in prison and you
know why. They say in the realm of France and else-

---

[46] *Chroniques de Froissart*, V, 64-5.
[47] *Ibid.*, III, 39-40.

where that you dare not let me go." The prince was so impressed by this argument that he immediately fixed a ransom for Bertrand's release.[48] As the constable was the only really effective commander the French possessed, sound military policy demanded that the prince follow his apparent inclination to keep him captive, but courtesy and reputation called for the other course. One could go on indefinitely illustrating the kindness of noble to noble from the pages of Froissart. One of the best examples comes from another source. A low class soldier had killed in battle the count of St. Pol. One day he was so indiscreet as to boast of this feat in the presence of his commander, the duke of Julliers, who had been St. Pol's bitter foe. The duke promptly had the fellow hanged for killing so noble a prince.[49] Mutual courtesy and class solidarity could go no farther than this.

The nobleman who wished to win fame as a knight could not afford to limit his efforts to the wars fought in his own country. Even in the midst of the Hundred Years War France knew brief periods of peace. While one could always arrange a series of jousts, these gentle knightly sports could not completely satisfy the more ardent spirits. To men intensely avid for martial glory crusades still offered promising opportunities. The favorite resort for French and English knights during lulls in their mutual hostilities was Prussia where the members of the Teutonic Order were gradually slashing Christianity into the native inhabitants. Among the

---

[48] *Ibid.*, VII, 62-3.
[49] *Chronique des quatre premiers Valois* (ed. Siméon Luce, Société de l'histoire de France, Paris, 1862), p. 218.

noted captains who made expeditions to Prussia were
Henry of Lancaster, earl of Derby, Duke Louis of
Bourbon, John de Grailly, captal de Buch, and Gaston
Phoebus, count of Foix. The Marshal Boucicaut made
three trips to this land of knightly exploits. The reader
may remember that Chaucer's knight "ful ofte tyme
hadde the bord bigonne aboven alle naciouns in Pruce."
Somewhat rarer because more difficult than excursions
to Prussia were crusades against the Moslem world.
Duke Louis of Bourbon led an abortive expedition to
aid the king of Castille against the Moors of Granada
and commanded an energetic if not very fruitful Franco-
Genoese invasion of north Africa. Many a glory-seeking
French knight including Boucicaut followed Count
John of Nevers, later duke of Burgundy, on his expedition against the Turks which ended in the disastrous
defeat at Nicopolis. Chaucer's emphasis on the foreign
adventures of his knight was in full accord with the
customs of the time. If a nobleman desired glory, he
had to seek opportunities for martial exploits.

The fifteenth century saw a gradual decrease both in
the practice of courtesy in war and in the importance of
desire for glory as a motive for fighting. Military tactics
and the composition of armies were changing to the
detriment of chivalry. The forces which followed
Henry V and his brother Bedford consisted of low-born
archers with a few gentlemen as officers. After the rout
of the chivalry of France at Agincourt, the cause of the
French king was supported for the most part by mercenary companies which rarely could boast of a noble
captain. Moreover while I have some hesitation about
subscribing to the common view that this stage of the

Hundred Years War saw a strong development of national feeling, it is certain that there was a bitterness between the contending parties which had been lacking in the fourteenth century. Henry V and Bedford were cold-blooded conquerors, not chivalrous adventurers, and their noble captains were professional soldiers who valued military success above chivalric glory. With the possible exception of Dunois and Richemont the French captains who eventually expelled the English were men of the same type as their foes. War had become a serious business. Duke Philip the Good of Burgundy might encourage jousts and tourneys as court amusements, but his armies were bodies of professional soldiers whose duty was to win battles. The days were past when generals cared little whether they won or lost so long as it was done gloriously.

The change in the nature of war was not the only force which tended to hamper chivalric practices. During the fourteenth century the nobles of France as a whole were rich and prosperous. They could afford to ask reasonable ransoms, to abstain from plundering, and to subordinate greed for profit to desire for glory. But the decrease in their resources and the expansion in the noble standard of living which marked the fifteenth century wrought a change in their attitude. Nobles began to hold gentlewomen for ransom—a thing practically unheard of in the fourteenth century. Others acted as captains of mercenary bands and cheerfully shared with their men in the plunder of the countryside. Still others entered élite regiments of the crown where one served frankly for pay as a permanent professional soldier. The nobles who banded against Louis XI in the

" League of the Public Weal " fought not for the traditional privileges of their class but for increased pensions
and offices in the royal government. Once more as in
the twelfth century the nobleman talked of glory but he
fought primarily for cash.

The conditions of the fifteenth century drove the
practice of courtesy and the search for glory from the
battlefield and forced them to take refuge in the martial
sports from which they had sprung. Among the nostal-
gic noblemen who tried to preserve the knightly practices of the past was many a forerunner of Don Quixote.
Adventurous young men wandered about Europe hope-
fully issuing challenges and finding few princes whose
romantic inclinations were strong enough to move them
to permit their subjects to joust with the challengers.
Now and then princely courts sought entertainment in
watching two massively armored knights tilt at each
other over a breast-high fence. But all this was pure
froth. The glory gained from such affairs was not for
prowess in battle but for reverence for tradition. The
noblemen whose real occupation was wheedling offices,
sinecures, and pensions out of kings and sovereign
princes still felt obliged to make their bow to the customs
of the past. The martial sports which had delighted the
knights of mediaeval France died on the field of Agincourt, but the corpse was not buried until Montgomery's
lance ended the reign of Henry II.

Such in brief was the history of the practice of feudal
chivalry in mediaeval France. Its connection with the
development of chivalric ideas is highly interesting but
quite intangible. Nevertheless it seems worth while to
venture a few rather reckless generalizations about the

relation between these ideas and their practice. In the period of growth ideas and practices seem to have developed together reacting one upon the other. The conditions of their environment induced scattered noblemen to behave in a certain manner. When this behavior had become fairly common and had persisted for a long time, men began to feel that it was peculiarly proper for noblemen. Then many nobles who might not otherwise have done so began to act in the same manner. Let us for instance assume that a fair number of late eleventh-century nobles found their resources greatly increased by the expansion of the arable land in their fiefs and were inclined to demonstrate their prosperity by lavish hospitality. Wandering minstrels and impecunious landless knights enjoyed the bounty of these laden tables and spread abroad the praises of their hosts. Less well endowed nobles felt called upon to be as lavish as their resources would permit. Soon hospitality on a generous scale became the mark of a nobleman and the chivalric virtue of *largesse* was fully developed. Thus the idea had its origin in practice but itself encouraged the spread of the practice. Ideas and practice grew side by side fertilizing each other.

The relation between ideas and practice in the period of decay was quite different from that which had prevailed in the period of growth. By the middle of the fourteenth century the noble class of France had accepted the ideas of feudal chivalry and was carrying them out in practice to a greater extent than at any earlier time. These ideas and practices had become the characteristic which in addition to high birth distinguished the nobleman. Rich townsmen who wished to ape the manners of the aristocracy made rather ludicrous attempts to hold jousts and tourneys. The complete identification of the ideas and practices of feudal chivalry with the dominant social class gave them an immense capacity for survival in the face of adverse conditions. Although the military, political, and economic conditions which formed the environment of the fifteenth-century nobleman were steadily growing less favorable to chivalric ideas and practice, the nobles clung desperately to what they and their contemporaries considered the true characteristics of their class. Hence during this period the popular conception of how a noble should behave definitely influenced the actions of the aristocracy and delayed the complete disappearance of chivalric practices. Caxton published the *Book of the order of chivalry* in the hope of reviving the knightly customs proper to noblemen. Henry VIII and Francis I held jousts at their courts because they felt that tradition demanded that nobles indulge in knightly sports.

III

RELIGIOUS CHIVALRY

WHILE the conditions of life in their natural habitat, the feudal court and the field of battle, were encouraging the nobles of France to develop the ethical ideas discussed in the last chapter, two alien environments, the cloister and the bedroom, were forcing other points of view on their attention. Churchmen and ladies were creating and propagating their own distinct and rather contradictory conceptions of the perfect nobleman. The first of these, the chivalric ideas propounded by ecclesiastics, will be the subject of this chapter. Since one of the chief functions of the church was to teach the Christian mode of life, there had, of course, been no time since the evangelization of the Teutonic barbarians when the clergy was not attempting to modify the ethical ideas and practices of the warriors of western Europe. They had tried to confine the robust lust of the Frankish aristocrats within the bounds of permanent monogamic marriage and had sought to curb their pride, avarice, and gluttony. Even more important from the point of view of society were the church's persistent efforts to reduce the aristocratic propensity to homicide and rapine or at least to mitigate its results. Although as early as the time of St. Augustine the church had modified its original abhorrence of all homicide to permit the killing of enemies and the execution of criminals at the command of a duly constituted authority, it steadfastly opposed the indiscriminate violence which marked the ninth and tenth centuries.[1] The direct line of attack on this evil, the attempt to persuade an aristocracy whose chief function was fighting that homicide should be abjured, was naturally not very fruitful, but the church made some progress in its efforts to mitigate the horrors of feudal warfare. The " Truce and Peace of God " forbade war on certain days and protected noncombatants such as clergy, women, merchants, and peasants. These edicts had some beneficial effect even when they were enforced only by the spiritual power of the church, and they furnished excellent programs for feudal princes like William the Conqueror who wished to establish order in their domains.[2] Then too by preaching the spiritual rewards that would be granted to those who fought the enemies of Christ the clergy moved many an eleventh-century noble to turn his martial energies against the Moslems who held Spain. In short from the sixth to the eleventh centuries the church strove to curb the typical vices of the warrior class or turn them into channels it approved. But during this period the exhortations of the clergy were addressed to the nobles as Christians who were bound as were all men to obey the laws of Christ. There was no suggestion that because a man was a noble he owed special obligations to the church and society. It was the appearance of this conception which seems to me to mark the beginning

[1] For an excellent discussion of the attitude of the early church fathers toward war see Gautier, *La chevalerie*, pp. 7-11.

[2] The best and most recent exposition of the effects of the " Truce of God " can be found in Julius Goebel, Jr., *Felony and misdemeanor* (New York, 1937), I, 297-328.

of religious chivalry. As long as the church simply maintained that a vicious noble was not a true Christian, its efforts and their results lie in the field of the historian of morals in general. Only when the clergy began to preach that a noble who violated certain rules was no true knight did its ideas come within the proper scope of the student of chivalry.

The earliest clear indication that I can find of the existence of this idea that a knight was peculiarly bound to obey and serve the church appears in the contemporary reports of the famous sermon with which in 1095 Pope Urban II roused the chivalry of Europe to undertake the First Crusade. While several of these reports definitely suggest this new conception of knighthood, a phrase in one of them expresses it unmistakably. " Now they may become knights who hitherto existed as robbers." [3] In other words the nobles who ignored the church's injunction to abstain from rapine were not knights. During the next fifty years after Urban's speech at Clermont-Ferrand I can find only two unequivocal references to this idea. Suger, abbot of St. Denis, while speaking of the notorious noble brigand Thomas de Marly states that a church council declared him unworthy to wear the belt of a knight.[4] William of St. Thierry, friend and biographer of Bernard of Clairvaux, in describing St. Bernard's father calls him a man of " ancient and legitimate chivalry." He made war according to the rules laid down by the church and

---

[3] *Patrologiae cursus completus, series latina* (ed. J. P. Migne, Paris, 1844-1864), CLI, 576.

[4] Suger, *Vie de Louis le Gros* (ed. Auguste Molinier, *Collection de textes pour servir à l'étude et à l'enseignement de l'histoire*, Paris, 1887), pp. 81-2.

abstained from plundering.[5] In this half century after
the First Crusade the chief expounder of the duties of
knights toward the church was, of course, Bernard himself, but his remarks on the subject were addressed to
the Templars. As the Templars were a military monastic
order, in Bernard's own words both knights and monks,
his injunctions to them cannot be taken as an expression
of his views on the duties and obligations of knights in
general. Hence the famous *De laude novae militiae* is
of little use to the historian of chivalry.[6] In fact the
employment of the word *novae* clearly implies that Bernard had no intention of restricting the term knight to
those who followed his precepts. Thus the first half of
the twelfth century furnishes little material to our purpose. It was not until after 1150 that ecclesiastical
writers began to expound their views on the proper
relations of knights to the church in extended and
orderly form.

The most distinguished and probably the earliest of
these mid-twelfth-century writers was the noted scholar
John of Salisbury. In the sixth book of his *Policraticus*
John presents a scathing criticism of the knights of his
day and expounds his views on the qualities knights
should possess and their proper function in society.[7] As
the minds of mediaeval men and particularly mediaeval
churchmen were deeply imbued with the sanctity of

[5] Migne, *Patrologia latina*, CLXXXV, 227.

[6] *Ibid.*, CLXXXII, 921-940.

[7] *Joannis Saresberiensis episcopi Carnotensis Policratici sive de nugis
curialium et vestigiis philosophorum* (ed. Clemens C. I. Webb, Oxford,
1909), II, 8-58. I have taken my quotations from the translation by
John Dickinson, *The statesman's book of John of Salisbury* (New
York, 1927).

custom and tradition, John felt called upon to produce authority and precedent for his conception of knighthood. He did this by making the twelfth-century *miles* or knight the successor to the Roman *miles* or legionary. The Roman legionary was a picked man, highly trained and rigidly disciplined, who was bound by a special oath to the service of the prince and the state. Hence men who were to be made knights should be carefully selected for soundness of blood, vigor of body, and courage of heart. Before receiving their belt of knighthood, they should take the " soldier's oath " to serve their prince loyally. As no one could serve a prince loyally who did not obey God and the church, this obligation was implied in the oath. These chosen and oath-bound men should then be rigorously trained in military science and bodily exercise. They should eschew luxury and display—should be temperate and chaste. Courage, hardihood, and knowledge of strategy and the use of arms should be their characteristics. If they failed to observe their oath or if they proved cowardly and incompetent, they should be deprived of their knightly belts and severely punished. The social function of knights is described by John with complete clarity.

But what is the office of the duly ordained soldiery? To defend the church, to assail infidelity, to venerate the priesthood, to protect the poor from injuries, to pacify the province, to pour out their blood for their brothers (as the formula of their oath instructs them), and, if need be, to lay down their lives. The high praises of God are in their throat, and two-edged swords are in their hands to execute punishment on the nations and rebuke upon the peoples, and to bind their kings in chains and their nobles in links of iron. But to what end? To the end that they may serve madness, vanity, avarice, or

their own private self-will? By no means. Rather to the end
that they may execute the judgment that is committed to them
to execute; wherein each follows not his own will but the
deliberate decision of God, the angels, and men, in accordance
with equity and the public utility.[8]

Despite the somewhat puzzling quotation from the
psalms the general purport of this statement is clear.
The knight should be a policeman bound to execute the
orders of church and state. Such in brief was John of
Salisbury's theory of chivalry. Some aspects of his ideas
require separate discussion.

John, of course, was fully aware that the term knight
in his day did not mean any specially selected man who
had taken a distinctive oath but simply an adult noble
who possessed complete military equipment. He solved
this difficulty as had Pope Urban. At the end of his
fiery denunciation of contemporary knights he said " For
it is nothing to the point if the men I have been speaking of walk crookedly, for such men are not under
military law because, if we speak accurately, none of
them is a true soldier." [9] In short only those who followed his precepts were true knights. The coward, the
brigand, the plunderer of churches, the oppressor of the
poor, the glutton, and the debauché were false knights
who should be deprived of the insignia of their rank.
Although John clearly has the conception of the " order
of knighthood "—an oath-bound brotherhood of chosen
men possessing certain qualities and admitting certain
obligations—he does not state this theory as definitely
as later writers. Still the implication is unmistakable.

[8] Dickinson, pp. 199-200.
[9] *Ibid.*, p. 190.

The military profession was instituted by God. Priests and knights are compared. " The former are called by the tongue of the pontiff to the service of the altar and the care of the church. The latter are chosen for the defence of the commonwealth by the tongue of the leader." [10] The two divinely instituted orders which play so important a part in chivalric literature are here in embryo. While this idea undoubtedly sprang from the well-known threefold division of mankind into fighters, prayers, and workers, it is not quite the same thing. John's clergy and knights are selected, consecrated groups, not mere subdivisions of humanity.

Naturally John of Salisbury's chief interest lay in emphasizing the obligations of knights toward the church. " This rule must be enjoined upon and fulfilled by every soldier, namely, that he shall keep inviolate the faith which he owes first to God and afterwards to the prince and the commonwealth." [11] John could not understand how any prince could trust a man who was unfaithful to his obligations to God and His church. He was also anxious to encourage the inclusion of some form of religious ceremony among those by which a man was made a knight. He spoke with approval of a custom by which a candidate for knighthood offered his sword to God on the altar of a church. While John referred to this usage as if it were a generally accepted practice in his day, we have ample evidence to show that it was by no means universal. John was simply encouraging what he considered a wholesome custom. He conceived of the knight as the special servant of church and

[10] *Ibid.*
[11] *Ibid.*, p. 201.

prince and felt that the ceremonies by which he was inducted into office should reflect both obligations.

The *Policraticus* contains all the essential features of religious chivalry. Later writers expanded the ideas and developed them in greater detail, but the general picture remained unchanged. A true knight must be courageous, hardy, and skilled in the use of arms, for fighting was his function in life. He must obey the commands of the church and use his sword in its defense. Finally he must serve his prince in defending the state and punishing criminals. His was the might that would enforce the laws of church and state. As John of Salisbury wrote in solemn scholarly latin, his words cannot be considered as direct propaganda addressed to knights. He was laying down a program for his ecclesiastical contemporaries, and it soon found expression in vernacular writings and popular sermons. One can hardly conceive of anyone reading the *Policraticus* aloud in a castle hall, but Stephen of Fougères' *Livre des manières* might well have entertained a reasonably serious-minded baron.[12]

Stephen of Fougères had been, as had John of Salisbury, a clerk attached to the court of King Henry II of England and through that monarch's patronage had become bishop of Rennes. Some scholars have maintained that he read the *Policraticus* and drew from it many of his ideas, but this seems far from certain. One can merely say that he was a contemporary and very

---

[12] *Estienne von Fougières' livre des manières* (ed. Josef Kremer, *Ausgaben und abhandlungen aus dem gebiete der romanischen philologie*, XXIX, Marburg, 1887), pp. 119-143. See also Ch. V. Langlois, *La vie en France au moyen âge de la fin du XIIe au milieu du XIVe siècle d'après des moralistes du temps* (Paris, 1925), pp. 1-26.

possibly an acquaintance of John of Salisbury and that both men used the same general fund of ideas. Stephen's *Livre des manières* consists of a diatribe against the ways of his time interspersed with moral advice. His views on chivalry were very similar to John's though expressed rather more definitely. A free man, born of a free mother, who had received the order of knighthood was bound to be effective in battle, brave, honest, loyal, and devoted to the church. He should not deny the church its tithes nor attempt to infeudate them. Unworthy knights should be deprived of their swords, have their spurs cut off, and be driven from the order. It should be noticed that Stephen emphasizes noble blood as a prerequisite for knighthood far more clearly than did John of Salisbury. Although John stated that knights should be of good family because such men were less likely to be cowards, his main interest was in their physical and mental fitness. Stephen assumed that a knight was a noble, a free man born of a free mother. Like John he insisted on the knights' obligations to the church and wished to deprive the unworthy of their rank. He definitely stated what John had merely suggested—that knights formed an order similar to that of the clergy. There were two swords, the spiritual and the temporal. The former had been given to clerks to excommunicate the wicked; the latter had been given to knights so that they might cut off the feet or hands of malefactors. The good of society demanded the cooperation of these two orders in wielding their swords against evil. Thus in this simple vernacular poem we have the ecclesiastical conception of chivalry expressed in a form that knights could comprehend.

While the *Livre des manières* was written in a lan guage and form that knights could understand, it seems unlikely that many nobles ever heard of it. Few knights could read, and despite its vigorous and pungent style this work can hardly have formed a part of the repertoire of wandering minstrels. For the successful propagation of their chivalric ideas the clergy were forced to seek other media. Probably the most effective course was to insert their teachings in songs and romances. At the very beginning of the twelfth century before ecclesiasti- cal chivalry had assumed definite form under the hands of St. Bernard and John of Salisbury many of its ideas appeared in the *Chanson de Roland*. Even if one does not accept M. Bédier's implication that this song was essentially a piece of advertising to attract pilgrims to the monasteries and shrines which lined the road to the tomb of St. James at Compostella, it is clear that most of the material for its composition was gathered from religious houses along that great pilgrimage route.[13] In the second half of the twelfth century the piety of old age and a religiously minded patron moved Chrétien de Troyes to produce *Perceval*.[14] The creator of Galahad, the author of the *Queste del Saint Graal*, was almost certainly a Cistercian monk.[15]

The *Chanson de Roland* is based on the conception of loyal service to God and the emperor. Roland fol- lowed his liege lord against the enemies of Christ and as he died he extended his right gauntlet toward the sky

[13] Joseph Bédier, *Les légendes épiques* (Paris, 1929), III, 289-360.
[14] Gustave Cohen, *Chrétien de Troyes et son oeuvre* (Paris, 1931), pp. 380-382.
[15] *La queste del Saint Graal* (ed. Albert Pauphilet, *Les classiques français du moyen âge*, Paris, 1923), pp. xiii-x.

in token of his vassalage to God. War against the infidel was one of the chief themes of the *chansons de geste*. Perceval and Galahad represent ecclesiastical chivalry expressed in terms of Arthurian romance. The latter divided his time about equally between performing heroic knightly deeds, resisting the advances of luscious ladies, and listening to moral discourses in monastic cloisters. In the earlier stories of the Arthurian cycle the knights roamed the world for the love of their ladies or in search of martial glory. The invention of the quest of the Holy Grail supplied a religious purpose for their activities. It would obviously be utterly reckless to state that Roland, Guillaume d'Orange, Perceval, Galahad, and the quest of the Holy Grail were invented in order to instill the ideas of religious chivalry in the nobles of France. One could argue equally plausibly that their existence in literature showed that these ideas were already popular among the knights and ladies for whom the stories were written. We can merely say that by finding their way into literature they forced themselves on the attention of the noble class.

One of the chief methods by which the church impressed its views on the laity was through sermons, and this medium was not neglected by the proponents of religious chivalry. Late in the twelfth or early in the thirteenth century Master Alan of Lille, perhaps the most celebrated scholar of his day, composed a short handbook for preachers. Among many model sermons he included one particularly addressed to knights. " For this purpose have knights been specially instituted—that they may defend their fatherland and ward off from the church the injuries of violent men. . . . They prostitute their knighthood who fight for profit. Those who take arms so that they may plunder are not knights but robbers and plunderers, not defenders but invaders." [16] It is, of course, impossible to say how often such sermons were actually preached, but it seems safe to assume that at least once in his life a knight would hear the religious conception of chivalry propounded from the pulpit.[17]

So far this chapter has consisted of a discussion of various ideas which churchmen of the eleventh and twelfth centuries were trying to instill in the minds of the nobles of France. There has been no attempt to describe a perfect knight according to the doctrines of religious chivalry, and this task would be essentially impossible. Except for St. Bernard whose words are inapplicable because they were addressed to the Templars no writer furnishes a complete picture of the ideal knight from a purely ecclesiastical point of view. The closest approach to such a work is *Le libre del orde de cauayleria* written by the Catalan Ramon Lull towards the end of the thirteenth century[18] After passing his youth at the court of the king of Aragon, Lull turned religious and devoted the remainder of his life to schemes for winning the Moslems to Christianity through missionary efforts. When he wrote his book on knighthood, Lull was a clergyman, but the fact that he had lived for

[16] Migne, *Patrologia latina*, CCX, 186.

[17] For fuller information about sermons addressed to knights see A. Lecoy de la Marche, *La chaire française au moyen âge* (Paris, 1886), pp. 385-397.

[18] I have used Caxton's English translation. Mr. Byles' introduction, which includes a detailed discussion of the differences between the versions, has enabled me to do so with confidence. *The book of the order of chivalry, translated and printed by William Caxton* (ed. Alfred T. P. Byles, *Early English text society*, London, 1926).

years as a lay gentleman influenced his views. Although
in general his conception of chivalry is in accord with
that of the church, his opinions would not have received
the full approval of John of Salisbury or Alan of Lille.
For instance John in common with most churchmen
abhorred tournaments, but Lull considers them a necessary part of a knight's activities. John frowned on
wordly glory as a motive for knightly deeds, while Lull
speaks of it as the only proper one for a true knight. The
former writes from the point of view of the church
alone, the latter from that of the knight as well. Hence
Lull's conception of chivalry is really a combination of
the feudal and religious. Nevertheless his emphasis on
the ideas propounded by the church seems to justify the
discussion of his work in a chapter devoted to religious
chivalry. There is no conclusive evidence as to how
popular Lull's book was in his own day, but by the
fifteenth century it had become the standard handbook
of chivalry. Originally written in Catalan it was translated into French by various writers who did not scruple
to modify and add to their original. Caxton translated
and printed one of these French versions while Sir Gil-
bert de la Haye rendered another into Scots. Caxton
presented his edition to King Richard III and suggested
that the king " command this book to be had and read
unto other young lords knights and gentlemen within
this realm that the noble order of chivalry be hereafter
better used and honored than it has been in late days
passed." [19] Caxton could not revive chivalry, but he did
place Lull's work in a dominant position among the
sources used by later English writers on the subject.

[19] *Book of the order of chivalry*, p. 125.

Lull's ideas about chivalry can be arranged for convenience in discussion under four general headings—the origin and nature of the order, its function, the qualities proper to a knight, and the education of aspirants to knighthood. As was becoming in one who wished to make a complete and orderly presentation of his subject Lull began his discourse on chivalry with an account of the origin of the order. In an age which traced the descent of both French and English from the exiled Trojans this description of the inception of chivalry was bound to be purely mythical: at a time when virtue had disappeared and vice reigned on earth God divided all men into thousands and in each group chose the most loyal, strongest, bravest, and best educated man to be a knight. Having supplied an exalted origin for chivalry Lull went on to discuss the nature and position of the order. Here the author's knightly background decidedly influenced his ideas. The dignity of the order of chivalry was so great that it was not enough that its members be chosen men equipped with the best of arms but they should enjoy eminent worldly rank as well. A knight should be lord over many men and should have a squire to care for him and his mount. The common people should work to support the knight so that he might live in complete economic security and pass his time in hunting and martial exercise. Ideally every knight ought to be master of a large territory and its inhabitants. Unfortunately there were too many knights, and only a few of them could be kings or great barons. Hence all temporal princes should choose only knights as their officers so that as many as possible of the order could enjoy the dignity to which they were entitled. Lull was

forced to admit that knights lacked the e
quired of a judge, but they were pre-eminer
all other offices. This is a fascinating piece
propaganda! Lull in common with the nobles of his day
resented the inclination of the feudal princes to fill their
administrative offices with obedient and tractable townsmen. In order to heighten still further the dignity of the
order Lull followed the tradition of comparing chivalry
and clergy. Knights and clerks held the two most honorable offices in the world and should cooperate with each
other in every way. As God instituted both orders, no
member of either one was justified in attacking the
other. The clergy urge the common people to virtue
by learning and example, while the knights accomplish
the same end by the terror inspired by their swords. In
short Lull maintained that the members of the divinely
instituted order of chivalry should be rich and powerful
nobles who combined with the clergy to enforce God's
will.

The function of the chivalric order was to supply the
force needed to maintain the laws of God and man. The
common people labored and cultivated the earth because
of their terror of the knights. The same dread made
them obey the laws of church and state. The knight's
first duty was to maintain and defend the Holy Catholic
Faith and the church that nurtured it. His second was
to maintain and defend his earthly lord and his native
land. His devotion to the church should lead him to
protect its special charges—women, widows, orphans,
and all the weak and helpless. His obligations to his
lord and country included not only their defense against
foreign foes but also the suppression of robbers and

criminals of all kinds. In order to keep in condition to perform his duties a knight should devote himself to martial exercise and noble sports. He should joust, tourney, and hunt wild beasts. Once more Lull's youth had its say. The obligations of his ideal knight were those envisaged by John of Salisbury and other ecclesiastical writers, but his exercises and diversions were those of the extremely imperfect nobles of the day. Lull could not counsel knights to abandon chase and joust.

The qualities which Lull considered requisite for a knight were a combination of martial and Christian virtues. The former were, of course, absolutely necessary. A knight had to be brave, strong of body, and skilled in the use of arms. Lull did suggest, however, that bravery was more effective when combined with intelligence. Then the knight should be courteous to all, keep himself well armed and well dressed, and maintain a suitable retinue. He should abjure perjury and lies, should be humble and chaste. Finally toward the end of his work Lull listed the Christian virtues and vices and showed how the former were necessary to and the latter destructive of a true knight. But martial and spiritual qualities were not enough for Lull's perfect knight. While he admitted that it was possible for new knightly lines to be founded by exceptional men, he emphasized the importance of noble birth. His translators dropped the qualification and enlarged on the rule. Beauty or at least normality of physique was another qualification—one who was lame, too fat, or in any way deformed should never be made a knight. Furthermore the knight had to be rich enough to maintain himself in the way of life proper to his place in society. Most important of all a true knight had to be actuated by a spirit of dedication. If he sought solely his own profit and honor rather than the reputation of the order as a whole, he was not fit to be a knight.

A large part of *Le libre del orde de cauayleria* is devoted to a discussion of the training of aspirants to knighthood and the ceremonies which should attend their reception into the order. As these questions concern the means of achieving the chivalric ideal rather than the ideas of chivalry, they are not entirely germane to my subject, but they are too interesting to be passed over. Lull expressed dissatisfaction with the contemporary method of training young nobles. The son of a knight was placed in a noble household where he acquired his knightly education while serving as page and squire. Lull criticized this eminently practical apprentice system not for inefficiency but for lack of dignity. Other professions, such as the religious, law, and medicine, were learned from books, and the military was entitled to equal consideration. He wanted the knowledge that was requisite for a knight reduced to writing so that aspirants could study it in schools of chivalry. On the basis of these statements Lull has been charged with expressing the utterly silly idea that skill in arms could be learned from books, but this does not seem justified. He did not want to abolish the period of apprenticeship. He merely wished to add to it some formal study in books. Furthermore it is clear from the early part of *Le libre del orde de cauayleria* that he considered this work a suitable textbook for young nobles who aspired to be knights. He did not conceive of having squires read books on the care of horses—such things they would learn by practice. It was the history of the chivalric order, its proper function in society, and the ethical principles which governed true knights that he wished the squires to study. In short Lull was partly the author encouraging the reading of his book and partly the enthusiast seeking to propagate an ideal. After his term of service as page and squire Lull wished the young noble to attend a school of chivalry where he would learn the duties and qualities of a true knight by reading *Le libre del orde de cauayleria*.

The chief interest in Lull's description of the ceremonies which should be performed when a man was made a knight lies in the prominent part given to the church. John of Salisbury and Stephen of Fougères had wished to have the aspirant to knighthood offer his sword on an altar as a token of his obligations to God and the church. Lull adds so many religious observances that the whole ceremony becomes decidedly ecclesiastical. On the day before he was to be dubbed a knight the young noble confessed. That night he passed in the church fasting and praying. In the morning he attended mass and listened to a sermon. The actual dubbing was performed while the squire knelt before the altar. The knight who was receiving him into the order girded on the novice's sword, kissed him, and gave him the ceremonial blow. Then the new knight rode through the town so that all could see him. That same day he gave a great feast for everyone who had attended the ceremony. Finally he and the knight who had dubbed him exchanged gifts and the heralds were duly feed. Again one seems to see Lull in a dual rôle. The solemn missionary to the Moslems described the formal ceremonies, but the gay young Catalan courtier planned the closing festivities.

One more aspect of Lull's book is worthy of mention— his discussion of the symbolical significance of the various articles which made up the equipment of a knight. The men of the Middle Ages were devoted to symbolism, but nowhere did this taste flourish more magnificently than among the ecclesiastical writers on chivalry. Every article of knightly equipment, even every part of an article, had its significance. True, no two writers were likely to attach the same meaning to an article, but this merely gave freer rein to the creative imagination. One of the earliest complete systems of symbolism for knightly arms was produced by Robert of Blois in his *Enseignement des princes*.[20] A few examples must suffice. The sword is clear and well polished—the knight should be honest and straight. The shield represents charity which covers many sins. The lance which pierces the foe before he gets near symbolizes foresight. Lull began his discussion of this subject by pointing out that every article of priestly vestments had its symbolic significance. Hence as knights were an order similar to the clergy, their equipment should also have a meaning. The sword is shaped like a cross. This signifies that knights should use the sword to slay foes of the cross. The sword has two edges to remind the knight that he should defend chivalry and justice. The shield symbolizes the office of a knight. As a knight places his shield between himself and his enemy, so a knight

---

[20] *Die didactischen und religiösen Dichtungen Robert's von Blois* (ed. Jacob Ulrich, Berlin, 1895), pp. 1-54. This is the third volume of Robert von Blois, *Sämmtliche werke*. See also Langlois, *La vie en France au moyen âge*, II, 184-194.

stands between prince and people. The knight should receive the blows aimed at his lord as his shield wards off those aimed at him. The lance represents truth, and its pennon marks the fact that truth fears not falseness. There is no need to go further. Enough has been said to show the general nature of this fascinating if rather fruitless pastime of inventing symbolic significance for the various pieces of a knight's equipment. Undoubtedly whenever an aspirant to knighthood followed Lull's precepts so far as to expose himself to a sermon before he was dubbed, he heard some priest's private version of what his equipment signified.

As the ecclesiastical conception of chivalry reached its fullest elaboration in *Le libre del orde de cauayleria*, there is no need to discuss the vast number of fourteenth and fifteenth-century works which dealt with all or part of the ideas which composed it. The continued popularity of Lull's book and the insignificance of the changes made in it by translators and adaptors show that the ideas of religious chivalry underwent no important modification during these two centuries. As our next step is to examine how completely these ideas were accepted and put in practice by the nobles of France, it seems well to summarize them here. The basic concept of religious chivalry was the idea that the true knight as distinguished from the ordinary nobleman recognized certain obligations to God and the church and that these true knights formed the order of chivalry which was closely similar in nature to the clerical order. Its members upheld the church and the faith against all their foes. They protected the helpless and suppressed the violent. Furthermore they practiced the

Christian virtues and obeyed the commands of the church in every respect. In short the ecclesiastical writers and preachers simply took those precepts of feudal chivalry that did not conflict with the teachings of the church and added to them certain ideas which they considered all important. The latter as summarized above formed the concepts peculiar to religious chivalry.

An examination into the extent to which a set of ideals was accepted by a class of society is an extremely difficult task especially when that class was in general illiterate and left few statements of its ideas and motives. Historians have been inclined to search for a practice in accord with an idea and then calmly assume that the idea furnished the motive for the practice. The usual treatment of the crusades is an illustration of this tendency. The crusades have been pointed to as evidence of the influence of church ideas of chivalry on the mind of the feudal noble. Now it is perfectly true that if a knight accepted the precept of religious chivalry that it was his chief duty to protect the church from its foes, he might well feel obligated to go on a crusade, but the fact that he became a crusader did not prove that he would have considered himself no true knight had he not done so. Many purely secular motives could impel a noble to join a crusade. A younger son might hope to conquer a fief from the Moslems. A baron hard pressed by his neighbors might hope to gain the church's aid and protection. An unsuccessful rebel might flee the wrath of his lord. A restless and war-loving young noble who lived in a district where some feudal prince was effectively suppressing disorder might go to Spain or the Holy Land in search of adventure and opportunities to fight. In fact one could go on almost indefinitely listing plausible secular reasons why a knight might undertake a crusade and illustrate each one with the case of a noble who apparently had that motive.

To turn to religious motives the most obvious was the desire for salvation or more exactly for the spiritual indulgences promised crusaders. But there was nothing essentially chivalric about this motive—salvation was the fundamental object of all Christian life. The influence of the religious conception of chivalry can only be demonstrated by showing that nobles went crusading because they believed that their reputations as good knights demanded it. Now this idea is not entirely absent from the few documents which apparently expressed crusading motives, the poems written by departing crusaders. Conan of Béthune, who took part in the crusade of 1189, pointed out to the ladies who were left at home that if they were unfaithful to their absent lovers they would sin with cowards and worthless men for all good men would be on the crusade.[21] An anonymous poem of about the same time stated that " God has called us to his aid and no worthy man should fail him." [22] Count Thibaut of Champagne was more explicit.

All the worthless will stay here, those who love neither God, nor the good, nor honor, nor worth. . . . Now they will go, the valiant bachelors who love God and the glory of this world, those who wisely wish to go to God, and the useless, the cowards will remain. Blind indeed is he who does not make

[21] *Les chansons de croisade* (ed. Joseph Bédier, Paris, 1909), pp. 32-36.
[22] *Ibid.*, pp. 69-72.

once in his life an expedition to succor God and who for so
little loses the praise of the world.[23]

The idea here is clear and definite. A noble who refused
to crusade deserved to be considered a worthless knight.

Although the ideas of religious chivalry had some
place in the minds of crusading nobles, no one who reads
Les chansons de croisade collected by M. Bédier can feel
that they had a very dominant influence. The search for
salvation was clearly the chief and usually the sole
religious motive. In this connection I cannot resist
quoting a most illuminating passage from the troubadour
Aimeric de Pégulhan.

> Behold! without renouncing our rich garments, our station in
> life, courtesy, and all that pleases and charms we can obtain
> honor down here and joy in Paradise. To conquer glory by
> fine deeds and escape hell; what count or king could ask more?
> No more is there need to be tonsured or shaved and lead a hard
> life in the most strict order if we can revenge the shame which
> the Turks have done us. Is this not truly to conquer at once
> land and sky, reputation in the world and with God? [24]

This may not represent the highest form of Christian
enthusiasm, but I suspect that it gives a fair picture of
the motives that moved most crusaders. In short while
I have little doubt that the ideas of religious chivalry
formed part of the mixture of reasons that led men to
leave their homes to fight the infidel, it seems unlikely
that chivalric conceptions were often the chief motives
and their presence is practically impossible to demonstrate. Knights sought to save their souls by founding

---

[23] *Ibid.*, pp. 171-173.
[24] Alfred Jeanroy, *La poésie lyrique des troubadours* (Paris, 1934),
II, 208.

monasteries, going on pilgrimages, and fighting Moslems, but this furnishes little or no evidence as to how far they had accepted the chivalric ideas expressed by such writers as John of Salisbury and Ramon Lull.

If one turns to the rest of the extremely scanty supply of documents which can be said to represent the views of the noblemen of France, one may find here and there indications of the existence of these ideas. For instance the conception that a knight should be a policeman for the church seems to have had some currency. The biographer of William Marshal felt that his hero had acted in knightly fashion when he plundered a renegade monk of money that the latter intended to loan at usury.[25] Joinville clearly approved of a knight who struck a Jew to the ground when he heard him uttering blasphemy.[26] There was also apparently a feeling that a knight should not harm religious personages. Froissart viewed the burning of abbeys and raping of nuns as decidedly unworthy of good knights.[27] The biographer of Marshal Boucicaut was much impressed by the Marshal's action in founding an order or fellowship of knights sworn to protect widows or other ladies in distress.[28] Undoubtedly such items could be multiplied, but the meagerness of the material available would prevent the formation of any reasonably sound generalization.

At the same time it is certain that some precepts of religious chivalry never gained any acceptance among the feudal class. Obviously no professional warrior was

[25] *Histoire de Guillaume le Maréchal*, I, lines 6677-6816.

[26] Jean, sire de Joinville, *Histoire de Saint Louis* (ed. M. Natalis de Wailly, *Société de l'histoire de France*, Paris, 1868), p. 19.

[27] *Chroniques de Froissart*, I, 171.

[28] *Livre des faicts du Maréschal de Boucicaut*, p. 255.

going to develop an abhorrence of homicide. The church prohibited tournaments, but they continued to be considered by the nobles of France as the most proper occupation for a knight. In fact the Avignon popes who lived under the dominance of the chivalrous kings of the Valois line felt obliged to rescind their predecessors' decrees against this form of knightly sport.[29] Finally it was useless for the church to preach against the taking of booty and ransoms. As William Marshal lay on his death bed, one of his knights pointed out to him that according to the teachings of the church no man could be saved who had not returned everything that he had taken from anyone. This did not worry the Marshal.

Henry, listen to me a while. The clerks are too hard on us. They shave us too closely. I have captured five hundred knights and have appropriated their arms, horses, and their entire equipment. If for this reason the kingdom of God is closed to me, I can do nothing about it, for I cannot return my booty. I can do no more for God than to give myself to him, repenting all my sins. Unless the clergy desire my damnation, they must ask no more. But their teaching is false—else no one could be saved.[30]

Perhaps William was unusual in daring to question the validity of the church's teaching, but most of his contemporaries must have shared his disregard of its precepts on this question. Certainly I can find no evidence that any feudal noble felt that homicide committed in

---

[29] H. Leclerq, *Histoire des conciles* (Paris, 1907-1921), V, I, 688; II, 1102. *Decretalium Gregorii papae IX*, liber V, titulus XIII, *Corpus juris canonici* (ed. Friedberg, Leipzig, 1879), II, 804. *Constitutiones Joannis papae XXII*, titulus IX, *ibid.*, 1215. See also Gautier, *La chevalerie*, pp. 681-2.

[30] Painter, *William Marshal*, pp. 285-6.

tourney or private war and the taking of booty and ransoms were anything but eminently proper in a knight.

As a matter of fact I am inclined to believe, though my evidence is quite tenuous, that the noble class abducted God from his position as founder and chief of religious chivalry and made him the patron of their own ideas on the subject. In the mind of Geoffrey of Villehardoin God was certainly on the side of the hardy knights who in defiance of the commands of pope, legate, and ordinary Christian decency captured the cities of Zara and Constantinople and had no use for the cowards who obeyed the church's order to go to Palestine. This was not, of course, very surprising. Soldiers have always been inclined to assume that God was on their side and have rarely failed to find priests to confirm their opinion. Particularly illuminating is the biographer of William Marshal's version of a speech delivered by Aimery de St. Maur, master of the Temple in England, as he stood by the bedside of the dying earl.

Marshal, attend. It pleases me that you give yourself to God. He has granted you a great favor—that you will never be separated from Him. He has shown you this in your life, and He will do the same after your death. In the world you have had more honor than any other knight for prowess, wisdom, and loyalty. When God granted you His grace to this extent, you may be sure He wished to have you at the end. You depart from the age with honor. You have been a gentleman and you die one.[31]

Add to this the words which the same author placed in the mouth of Stephen Langton, archbishop of Canterbury, as he preached the Marshal's funeral sermon:

[31] Painter, *William Marshal*, pp. 284-5.

Behold all that remains of the best knight who ever lived. . . .
We have here our mirror, you and I. Let each man say his
paternoster that God may receive this Christian into His Glory
and place him among His faithful vassals, as he so well
deserves.[32]

Now William Marshal was no devotee of the ideas of
religious chivalry. He had passed his life in industrious
homicide in tourney and battle. For years he lived on
ransoms won in tournaments. True, he had founded
monasteries, but he had also plundered bishops. As
these eloquent eulogies were being pronounced he lay
under an excommunication launched by the bishop of
Kilkenny. There can be no doubt that his biographer
knew all this. To that anonymous writer who was so
thoroughly imbued with the ideas of feudal chivalry
it seemed impossible that God should not appreciate the
virtues of a good knight. Prowess, wisdom, loyalty,
generosity—what more could God ask?

On the whole it seems clear that the ideas of religious
chivalry were current among the nobles of mediaeval
France and may to some slight extent have modified
their ethical conceptions. But it is certain that they
never became so dominant in the feudal mind that the
ideal of knighthood propounded by the church replaced
the one developed by the knights themselves. The men
of the thirteenth, fourteenth, and fifteenth centuries
who were admired by their contemporaries as models of
knighthood were not perfect knights according to the
ecclesiastical ideas. St. Louis who probably came as
close to the church ideal as a living king could was
admired as monarch and saint rather than as a knight.

[32] Painter, *William Marshal*, p. 289.

It was men like King Philip of Valois and his son John the Good, the Black Prince, and Bertrand du Guesclin who were considered the best knights of their day. In short the religious conception of chivalry made some impression on the mind of the feudal caste, but it never gained mastery over it. The virtues of feudal chivalry remained the qualities that were admired in a knight.

Obviously if I am correct in my belief that the ideas of religious chivalry made only a slight impression on the ethical conceptions of the nobility, they cannot have had much effect on its practices. Of course one could list an enormous number of nobles who went on crusades, but as I have attempted to show in a previous paragraph it is not necessary to believe that these ideas played any great part in persuading them to do so. Then most knights accepted without question the faith preached by the church and observed more or less carefully the established forms of the Christian cult. Many knights were pious, devout, and obedient Christians. But this could be said of the nobles of the eighth, ninth, and tenth centuries—it has little to do with chivalry. If the religious ideas of chivalry had ever been extensively practiced, one would expect to find a time when knights refrained from rapine and casual manslaughter, protected the church and its clergy, and respected the rights of helpless non-combatants in war. I can find no evidence that there ever was such a period. Many writers on the subject, both mediaeval and modern, have postulated a " golden age of chivalry " when the church's precepts were rigorously observed. Usually this glorious era has been placed in the twelfth century.[33] Unfortu-

[33] See Raymond L. Kilgour, *The decline of chivalry as shown in the*

nately twelfth-century writers like John of Salisbury and Stephen of Fougères were loud in their denunciations of the knights of their day, and other evidence thoroughly corroborates their statements. A case of some sort might be made for the claim that less regard was shown for human life and the persons and property of clergy and non-combatants in the fourteenth and fifteenth centuries than in the twelfth and thirteenth, but it would not be very convincing as a manifestation of chivalric decline. While it is possible to cite many more atrocities from the Hundred Years War than from the earlier period, one must remember that there is much more information available about the events of the later era. Then too the increase in the use of non-noble professional soldiers undoubtedly intensified the horrors of war. There seems no sound reason for believing that the knights of the later Middle Ages observed the precepts of the church any less scrupulously than had their predecessors. In only one respect can one find evidence of definite variation in practice. From the middle of the twelfth century to the middle of the thirteenth the lives of noblemen appear to have been sacred except on the field of battle or the tourneying ground. Assassination and execution for political or criminal offenses was so rare as to be practically unknown. I can advance no explanation of this interesting phenomenon unless it be that the newly developed solidarity of the feudal caste had not yet succumbed to political necessities. At any rate there is no reason for connecting it with religious

French literature of the late Middle Ages (Cambridge, Massachusetts, 1937), pp. 4-5. Although he is fully aware of contemporary criticisms of knights, Mr. Kilgour places the great age of chivalry in the twelfth century.

chivalry. Thus while it seems likely that individual knights were occasionally influenced in their practice by the ideals of chivalry propagated by churchmen, no grounds exist for believing that these ideas changed the behavior of the nobility as a whole. Religious chivalry as expressed by the writers of the Middle Ages has always appealed strongly to romantically inclined lovers of mankind. Virtue combined with might is perennially attractive. Nevertheless it seems probable that this fascinating conception was never much more than a pleasant dream.

IV

COURTLY LOVE

While the clergy was bombarding the noblemen with the precepts of religious chivalry, the ladies of France were carrying on a more effective campaign of propaganda in favor of their conception of the ideal knight. Few ladies could write, but all could dispense good dinners, fine clothes, and rich gifts to the wandering minstrels who supplied the feudal caste with its literary entertainment. Hence the nobles were continually exposed to the ideas of courtly love which came to them neatly concealed among the tales of battles and tourneys which were the delight of their long evenings. This creation of the ladies and their allies the minstrels is in at least one respect the most interesting of the three sets of chivalric ideas. Feudal chivalry was simply the spontaneous development of the immemorial warrior virtues under the influence of mediaeval conditions. Religious chivalry grew naturally out of St. Augustine's conception of the Christian soldier. As complete concepts both were products of mediaeval life, yet their component ideas were not new. Courtly love, on the other hand, was essentially novel. The romantic aura which has always surrounded the relations between men and women, waxing and waning in accord with contemporary conditions, was given a new form by the courtly writers. To them love was neither the god-sent

95

madness that caused the siege of Troy and dogged the footsteps of Odysseus and Aeneas nor the highly cultivated appetite which gave so much pleasure to the Hellenistic lyric poets and their Roman successors. Courtly love was to its adherents the most vital element of noble life—the source of all noble virtues. Love and lust are as old as the human race, but *fin amour* was essentially a product of the Middle Ages.

The ideas about sexual ethics which were current among the nobles of the ninth and tenth centuries were the product of their cultural tradition and environment somewhat modified by the teachings of the church. Unfortunately the ideas of the Teutonic barbarians on this subject are very obscure. Tacitus is explicit in his praise of the high level of sexual morality maintained by the Germans, but the reliability of his account is open to grave doubts. It has been suggested that Tacitus' purpose was to contrast the loose customs of his fellow Romans with those of an imaginary noble savage, the simple barbarian German. His picture is in accord neither with what one would expect from a people in the stage of civilization which had been reached by the Germans nor with what we know of the Germans themselves four centuries later. The only evidence which seems to corroborate Tacitus comes from the eighth century apostle to the Germans, St. Boniface, who in a letter to an Anglo-Saxon monarch praises the moral virtues of the ancient Saxons.[1] But when one attempts to speculate as to where Boniface got his information about the ancient Saxons, one is forced to conclude that

[1] *Die briefe des heiligen Bonifatius und Lullus* (ed. Michael Tangl, *Monumenta Germaniae historica, Epistolae selectae*, I, Berlin, 1916), pp. 150-151.

he had been reading Tacitus. Gregory of Tours and other writers who knew the Franks in Merovingian and Carolingian times make it clear that their monarchs and great men were no models of Victorian propriety. Few Merovingian rulers made any distinction between concubines and wives both of which they kept in generous numbers. Even the great Charlemagne, while refusing to allow his daughters to marry because of his fear of the political influence of sons-in-laws, cheerfully permitted them to bear children to various dignitaries of his court. A dozen instances scattered over three centuries cannot, however, be taken as a reliable indication of the customs of a people. Some information of wider applicability may be gleaned from the Germanic law codes. These make clear that women were protected from violence to their modesty and that such violence was assumed to be a common occurrence. For instance the *Leges Alamannorum* provided that if a man met a free woman in the country and deprived her of all that she wore above the waist, he had to pay a penalty of six solidi. If he stripped her entirely, the composition was doubled and if he raped her, he paid a penalty of forty solidi.[2] These codes clearly considered adultery and wife stealing as serious offenses. Women were valued as property and particularly as child-bearers. The *Lex Ripuaria* set the penalty for killing a free woman between the age of puberty and her fortieth year at six hundred solidi, while the death of a young girl cost only two hundred. As the code estimated six hundred solidi to be the equivalent of three hundred cattle or

[2] *Leges Alamannorum* (ed. Karl Lehman, *Monumenta Germaniae historica, Leges nationum Germanicarum*, V, part 1, Hanover, 1888), p. 115.

fifty male horses, this was an extremely heavy penalty and provision was made for its payment in installments extending over three generations.[3] In general the codes indicate that wives were expected to be chaste, that marriage was easily dissolved, and that concubinage was prevalent. We are left with a picture of the Germans as brutal, lustful people who objected to adultery with their wives or violence to their daughters as serious infringements on their property rights.

The environment of the feudal class in the tenth and eleventh centuries tended to confirm the conception of sexual ethics which they had inherited from their ancestors. The sole interest of the feudal noble which transcended his own pleasure in this world or the next was the fief which he had built up or maintained. His great desire was to have an heir worthy to succeed him in his estates. Now the men of the Middle Ages had no doubt that all traits were inherited and that a good soldier must come from the blood of good soldiers. In this connection it is interesting to note that from the time of the early Germanic codes down through the entire mediaeval period the adultery committed by a wife with a social inferior was a peculiarly heinous offense. This idea was expressed very clearly by the troubadour Marcabrun. Cowardly and niggardly barons were, he believed, the product of their mothers' adulteries with varlets.[4]

---

[3] *Lex Ribuaria* (ed. Rudolph Sohm, *Monumenta Germaniae historica, Legum*, V, Hanover, 1875-1879), pp. 216-217, 231.

[4] *Leges Visigothorum* (ed. Karl Zeumer, *Monumenta Germaniae historica, Leges nationum Germanicarum*, I, Hanover, 1902), pp. 133-135. *Lex Ribuaria*, p. 246. *Poésies complètes du troubadour Marcabru* (ed. Dejeanne, *Bibliothèque Méridionale*, XII, Toulouse, 1909), p. 150. See also poem by Bertrand de Born in Anglade, *Anthologie des troubadours*, p. 60.

But even when the offense was committed with a nobleman, the biological theories of the day held small hope
for the offspring of adulterous unions. A child was
produced from the merging blood of father and mother.
Hence a child of adultery would come from mixed and
confused blood, that of the mother, her husband, and
her lover. The result was bound to be a worthless man
who was no fit heir to a baron.[5] This magnificent scien-
tific confirmation of ecclesiastical doctrines may have
served also to strengthen a traditional inclination on the
part of the nobles to demand virgin brides though one
finds difficulty in reconciling current theory with the
highly prevalent practice of marrying rich widows. At
any rate feudal customary law insisted on the chastity
of wives and young girls. If a husband suspected his
wife of infidelity, he could warn her and her supposed
lover and if he found them together after the warning,
he was allowed to kill both of them. If a noble considered anyone a menace to the chastity of his daughter,
he could forbid him to approach her and slay him if he
violated the prohibition. While a father was not permitted to take the life of an erring daughter, a girl who
allowed herself to be deprived of her virginity lost all
share in the family inheritance. If a man who had been
intrusted with the guardianship of a young girl seduced
her, he lost his fief. If he raped her forcibly, he was to
be hanged.[6] The same interest in the future of their

[5] *Hildegardis causae et curae* (ed. Paul Kaiser, Leipzig, 1903), pp.
68-9.
[6] Philippe de Beaumanoir, *Coutumes de Beauvaisis* (ed. Salmon,
Paris, 1899), I, 472-3. *Coutume de Touraine-Anjou* in *Les établisse-
ments de Saint Louis* (ed. Paul Viollet, Société de l'histoire de France,
Paris, 1883), III, 5, 26.

fiefs which moved the nobles to protect so rigidly the chastity of their wives and daughters made them very tenacious of their right to dissolve unsatisfactory marriages. If his wife supplied no male heir, the knight wished to be free to replace her with one that would. Furthermore if the interests of the noble and his fief seemed to demand a certain marriage alliance, he was unwilling to be unduly hampered by the fact that he already had a wife. The documents of the Frankish period show that marriage could easily be dissolved by mutual consent.[7] By the tenth and eleventh centuries the influence of the church seems to have eliminated this process from formal customary law, but repudiation of wives was still a common practice. Not until the latter part of the twelfth century did the church seriously threaten the noble's right to marry and repudiate at will and then it did little more than gain some control over the practice by insisting that it be accomplished through a formal action in its courts.

Besides tending to make marriage sacred and at the same time impermanent the conditions of feudal life encouraged the use of concubines. The noble chose his wife because of her family connections, her marriage portion, and her ability to bear sons. Beauty, charm, and compatibility rarely entered into the matter. As a result the nobleman was inclined to satisfy his lust where he found the process most pleasant. While there seems to have been a feeling that a man whose wife was beautiful and charming had less excuse than others to seek his

---

[7] *Formulae Merowingici et Karolini aevi* (ed. Karl Zeumer, *Monumenta Germania historica, Leges*, V, Hanover, 1886), pp. 94, 145-6, 248.

pleasure elsewhere, outside of the ranks of the clergy concubinage was taken as a matter of course. The imposing number of bastards mentioned in the documents of the period shows how thoroughly the nobles appreciated their mistresses. Moreover the feudal courts were usually well supplied with prostitutes. If retrospective evidence from the late thirteenth century is to be believed, the constable of Chester in England had a vassal who was a sort of master of the revels and controlled all the minstrels and prostitutes in his fief. The same material indicates that the manor of Catteshall in Surrey was held of the English king by the service of being the marshal of the court prostitutes.[8] Many anecdotes show clearly that light women were assumed to be an important element in French feudal households. We even hear of women of noble birth who drifted into this widely-patronized profession.[9]

Although generalizations are always dangerous and the makers of them must be prepared to meet the citation of innumerable exceptions, it seems safe to say that the conditions which governed the life of the feudal class forced women to occupy a low place in society. The supreme function of the noble was war, and women could not fight. Although as time went on the attitude of feudal law toward women steadily improved, they were never accorded many rights. In the early feudal period most fiefs could not be inherited by women—a condition which persisted in Germany. In France by

[8] *Calendar of inquisitions post mortem* (*Rolls series*), III, 145, 506.
[9] Caesarius of Heisterbach, *The dialogue on miracles* (translated by Scott and Bland, *Broadway medieval library*, London, 1929), II, 200-201. *Anecdotes historiques d'Etienne de Bourbon*, pp. 393-4.

the twelfth century daughters could inherit when there were no sons, but their control of the fief was greatly restricted. Not until the thirteenth century was it customary to allow a woman to do or receive homage. A woman was never her own mistress and could exercise her inherited privileges only through her husband or guardian. If she were unmarried she was in the care of her father or if he were dead of a guardian designated by custom. Once she was married, she and her lands were at the disposal of her husband. In case she became a widow, she fell once more into custody. A woman could not sue in court except through the male in whose charge she was at the time. Some feudal codes allowed her to bring a criminal action in the case of rape of herself or the murder of her husband in her presence, but often she needed a guardian to act even in these cases. In short at law the woman was always a minor in the tutelage of some male.

The feudal male was chiefly absorbed in war and the chase. His wife bore him sons, his mistress satisfied his momentary lusts. Beyond this women had no place in his life, and he had no interest in them. They were freely beaten and treated in general with callous brutality. The *chansons de geste* show very clearly the attitude of the twelfth-century knight toward women. As these works were obviously composed with a male audience chiefly in mind, they emphasized what the nobleman liked. For the most part they dealt with war and feudal intrigue, but occasionally a woman slipped into the story. Some were noble and virtuous wives and mothers. They appeared nursing their children, mourning their slain husbands, and exhorting their sons to brave and often cruel deeds. They were the victims of savage indignities. If a wife opposed her husband, his usual reply was to hit her on the nose so that it bled. The emperor calmly told the wife of one of his rebellious barons that if she did not accept a different husband at his command he would turn her over to his varlets for their amusement.[10] But on the whole little space was devoted to these worthy ladies—they simply did not interest the knightly listeners. The only women who received any great amount of attention were beautiful and sensual young girls of exalted rank, usually Christian or Moslem princesses. Apparently the favorite diversion of the former was to slip into the beds of unsuspecting and often not very receptive male guests. The Moslem princesses invariably removed the handsome Christian captives from their fathers' dungeons and entertained them luxuriously and lasciviously in their own apartments. From the point of view of the composers of the *chansons* the great advantage of using Moslem ladies lay in the fact that eventually they could be converted. The baptism of a fair Saracen gave scope to their best lyrical efforts. The lady could be undressed and her charms and their effect on the knightly onlookers described in great detail all with the pious and worthy object of recounting a solemn religious ceremony.[11] These entertaining but shameless girls profoundly shocked Léon Gautier, the historian of chivalry as portrayed in the *chansons*. As Gautier was firmly convinced that these songs gave an accurate picture of

[10] *Raoul de Cambrai*, p. 213.

[11] For a peculiarly vivid description of a baptism see *Fierabras* (ed. Kroeber and Servois, *Les anciens poetes de la France*, Paris, 1860), p. 181.

feudal life, he was faced with the conclusion that young
noblewomen actually behaved that way. He finally
extricated himself by saying that while the authors of
the *chansons* knew all about knights, they had very little
knowledge of young girls.[12] Obviously no such dubious
hypothesis is needed to protect the reputation of the
maidens of mediaeval France. The girls of the *chansons*
did not necessarily represent young noblewomen as they
were but as the males would have liked them to be. As
a matter of fact these minxes rarely married the knights
on whom they lavished their favors. They were either
calmly deserted or passed off on secondary characters
in the story. The composer of the songs dealt with what
the knights of the day were interested in—war, feudal
intrigue, and light women. A high-born virgin burning
with desire to climb into his bed has probably always
been a favorite subject for man's daydreams.

The cultural tradition, environment, and natural
inclinations of the brutal and vigorous feudal male were
not the sole forces that governed the sexual ethics of the
noble class. For some six hundred years the aristocracy
of France had been exposed to the teachings of the
Christian church. The attitude of the church on the
proper relations between the sexes is too well known to
require extended discussion. All sexual intercourse outside the bond of marriage was mortal sin, and even
within marriage intercourse was lawful only when its
purpose was to beget children. The early church fathers
seem to have considered intercourse between a husband
and wife who did not desire children as mortal sin, but
later writers reduced it to a venial offense. A spouse

[12] Gautier, *La chevalerie*, pp. 377-379.

who submitted in order to prevent the other from sin-
ning elsewhere was blameless.[13] In brief the church
opposed all extra-marital relations and those between
husband and wife when not motivated by a desire for
progeny. The church also maintained vigorously the
doctrine of indissoluble, life-long marriage. Whenever
it felt strong enough, it attempted to curb the casual
repudiations which were so common in the noble class.
While it is true that the church's decrees which prohibited marriages among relatives were a highly con-
venient means of annulling an unsatisfactory union, the
church as a whole did not connive at their use for this
purpose whatever individual ecclesiastics might feel
compelled to do at the behest of a great lay lord. The
church's attitude toward women in general was ambigu-
ous. The clergy sought to protect them from brutality.
Canon law forbade a man to beat his wife with unreasonable severity. The " Truce and Peace of God " de-
creed the immunity of women from the horrors of feudal
war. Many theologians and preachers maintained that
the fact that God had created woman from man's rib
rather than from some lower member such as a foot
proved that He intended her to be man's equal. But the
ascetic tendencies of Christianity impelled the church
to consider woman the original source of sin and a weak
vessel peculiarly liable to vice. Her mere existence
tempted men to sins of the flesh and her inclinations
to provocative behavior increased the menace. Moreover
the actual position of woman in contemporary society

[13] This subject was thoroughly discussed by St. Thomas Aquinas.
Somme théologique de S. Thomas d'Aquin (edited and translated by
F. Lachat, Paris, 1880), XV, 117-19.

was bound to influence the ideas of ecclesiastical writers. Thomas Aquinas held that she was ordained to be completely subject to man. As man stood to God, so stood woman to man.[14]

Nevertheless serious as the disabilities were that burdened the noblewomen of eleventh-century France their position gave them the means through which they could improve their status. Roman and Germanic tradition had combined with the primitive conditions of contemporary life to save women from the deep degradation of confinement in a harem under the custody of servants. The noblewoman was completely subject to her husband, but under his hegemony she was mistress of the household. The women performed their tasks and the younger children received their training under her supervision. The knight's wife was a recognized member of the family partnership. In the *chansons de geste* the wife whose advice displeased her husband was frequently rewarded by a savage blow, but this must not be allowed to obscure the very important fact that she felt fully competent to express her views. Moreover in the absence of her husband the lady was no mere valuable chattel in the care of his military or administrative deputies but the actual mistress of the castle and the fief. In both history and romance ladies appear directing the defense of their strongholds against besieging hosts. The noblewoman was the absolute dependent of her husband, and her relations with the outside world could only be conducted through him, but she enjoyed a posi-

---

[14] For an excellent discussion of this very complicated question see Bede Jarrett, *Social theories of the middle ages* (Boston, 1926), pp. 70-73.

tion of dignity and authority in the community of which
he was the head. Vassals, servants, and wandering
minstrels might well seek the favor of the lady of the
castle.

The nature and the essential novelty of the ideas of
courtly love which appeared in France early in the
twelfth century can best be shown by an illustration
from the literature of the time. I am going to place
before the reader abbreviated versions of two courtships—that of Amiles and Charlemagne's daughter from
Amis et Amiles and that of Alexander and Soredamors
from *Cligès*. The latter was written by Chrétien de
Troyes who was deeply imbued with the conceptions of
romantic love, while the author of the former made no
use of courtly ideas. Obviously it would be highly con-
venient to be able to say that *Amis and Amiles* which
shows no sign of the new theories of love was the earlier
of the two works, but unfortunately this does not seem
to be the case. The old and the new ideas flourished
side by side, and *Amis and Amiles* was written some
thirty years later than *Cligès*.[15]

The scene from the former work starts with Count
Amiles staying as a guest at Charlemagne's court. The
emperor's daughter approached him. " Sire " she said
" I love none but you. Summon me into your bed some
night: my whole body will be at your disposal." The
count politely declined this generous offer. That night
he slept in a great bed of crystal and sapphire in a room
lighted with a large candelabra. The girl looked into
the room and said to herself " Ha! God, good father of

---

[15] Karl Voretzsch, *Introduction to the study of old French literature*
(translated by Francis Du Mont, New York, 1931), pp. 217, 278.

hope! Whoever saw a man of such proud vassalage, of such prowess, of such baronage who deigned neither to love me nor to look at me . . . No woman ever was so keen to go into his bed at night. I shall lie down under his marten skins. I do not care what people think nor if my father beats me daily, for he is too handsome a man." At midnight the princess got up, went to the count's bed and slipped in beside him. This disturbed Amiles. "Who are you who lies with me at such an hour? If you are a married woman or Charlemagne's daughter, I conjure you by Christ the son of Mary, my sweet friend, to go back where you belong. If you are a chambermaid of low rank, stay with me and you shall have a hundred sous in the morning." [16] The rest of the scene is rather too intimate for repetition, but enough has been given to show the general nature of the courtship.

Let us turn to *Cligès*. Alexander is visiting the court of King Arthur and accompanies that monarch and his queen on a trip to Brittany. The queen has among her maidens Soredamors, a beautiful and charming girl who has no use for love. As soon as they see each other on the boat, Alexander and Soredamors fall in love. The queen notices that they lose color, grow pale, sigh, and shudder, but she thinks they are merely seasick. From that moment love grows in them both. As Chrétien says, "Their love grows and increases continually: but the one feels shame before the other, and each conceals and hides his love so that neither flame nor smoke is seen from the coal beneath the ashes." But both can bemoan their fate at night. Alexander does so for two

[16] *Amis et Amiles* (ed. Konrad Hofmann, Erlangen, 1882), pp. 19-21.

hundred and fifty odd lines and Soredamors is in no
better state. " All night she is in so great pain that she
neither sleeps nor rests. Love has set in array within
her a battle that rages and mightily agitates her heart,
and which causes such anguish and torture that she
weeps all night, and complains and tosses and starts up,
so that her heart all but stops beating." She then complains for a hundred and fifty lines. Apparently the two
lovers spent some three months in this deplorable state.
Eventually word comes to Arthur that England is in
revolt, and he decides to knight Alexander so that he
may aid him to crush the rebels. The queen is anxious
to give the new knight a fine shirt and searching in her
chests finds one sewed entirely with golden thread.
Soredamors had done the sewing and had woven strands
of her golden hair with the threads. One evening as
Alexander sits in the hall by the queen she notices the
mingled threads and hairs and calls for Soredamors to
explain the unusual sewing. " Alexander was much
joyed when he saw her approach so near that he could
have touched her, but he has not so much courage as to
dare even to look at her, but all his senses have so left
him that he has almost become dumb. And she, on the
other hand, is so bewildered that she has no use of her
eyes, but fixes her gaze on the ground and dares not
direct it elsewhere." Soredamors admits the hairs are
hers, and that night Alexander sleeps with the shirt in
his arms. Apparently if left to themselves Alexander
and Soredamors might have gone on suffering for ever,
but the queen took pity on them. She called both to her,
told them that she knew they were in love, and offered

to arrange their marriage.[17] Thus ended a thoroughly courteous courtship.

The ideas of courtly love first appeared in the lyric poetry composed by the troubadours of southern France. The origins of this poetry have been the subject of endless scholarly controversy. It now seems well established that long before the appearance of the troubadours there were in this pleasant region wandering minstrels who were acquainted with the verse forms which were to be used by their better known successors. Unfortunately the student of chivalry is concerned not with verse forms but with ideas, and here one can do little more than guess. There are two important schools of thought on the question. One holds that the troubadour ideas about love grew spontaneously out of the environment supplied by southern France in the eleventh and twelfth centuries. The other contends that the origin of these ideas must be sought in the Arabic lyric poetry of Moslem Spain. Alfred Jeanroy, the most distinguished modern student of the subject, makes an alluring case for the first hypothesis, but his arguments against the other are far from convincing.[18] While I am inclined to believe that Jeanroy is right, I should not be surprised if someone were to present overwhelming evidence in favor of the other theory. Until more has been done by scholars who are masters of both Arabic and Provençal, the question must remain open. Let us then accept the position of Jeanroy and using his theory as a basis go into the realm of pure conjecture in an attempt

[17] Chrétien de Troyes, *Cligés* (translated by F. Gardiner, *The new medieval library*, New York, 1912), pp. 12-62.
[18] Jeanroy, *La poésie lyrique des troubadours*, I, 61-100.

to describe the circumstances which surrounded the beginnings of troubadour poetry.

One day toward the middle of the eleventh century a very hungry minstrel who was wandering about the duchy of Aquitaine came to a castle where he hoped that his tales of battles, broad stories, and tumbling tricks would earn him a good dinner. Unfortunately he found the lord absent and the lady heartily tired of hearing about endless battles. Then it occurred to the minstrel that if he composed a song in praise of the lady's beauty and virtue and described their effect on him in glowing terms, he might get the dinner after all. The experiment was successful, and soon the minstrel was recommending the same course to his colleagues. It was not long before the baronial halls of southern France were ringing with songs in praise of ladies who were able to dispense lavish hospitality. If a lady did not have a minstrel singing her virtues, she felt definitely out of fashion. Then one day a great and lusty lord, William IX, count of Poitou and duke of Aquitaine, heard one of the songs and decided to turn his hand to composing love lyrics. He had no need to sing for his dinner. His purpose seems to have been to furnish a pleasant accompaniment to his numerous triumphs over feminine virtue and then to regale his boon companions with songs recounting his amorous victories.[19] The poetic activities of this mighty feudal prince, the suzerain of a third of France, soon set the fashion. A baron of the south felt that his prestige demanded that he sing songs in praise of a lady. If this was completely beyond his talents, he could at least

---

[19] *Les chansons de Guillaume IX, duc d'Aquitaine* (ed. Alfred Jeanroy, *Les classiques français du moyen âge*, Paris, 1927).

patronize poor poets. Thus the singing of love lyrics became a fad. Barons and knights sang because it was pleasant and fashionable, poor minstrels because they had to live.

The fundamental idea which formed the basis for the lyric poetry of the troubadours was their conception of love. To them love was the emotion produced by unrestrained adoration of a lady. Love might be rewarded by smiles, kisses, or still higher favors, but their presence or absence had no essential effect on love itself. All the benefits and torments which came to the lover grew out of simple worship of a lovely and worthy woman. This love was caused by the lady's good qualities—her beauty, charm, wit, and character. " The great beauty, the good manners, the shining worth, the high reputation, the courteous speech, and the fresh complexion which you possess, good lady of worth, inspire me with the desire and the ability to sing." [20] Once aroused this emotion had tremendous effects on the lover. " My heart is so full of joy that everything in nature seems changed. I see in the winter only white, red and yellow flowers; the wind and rain do nothing but add to my happiness; my skill waxes and my song grows better. I have in my heart so much love, joy, and pleasure that ice seems to me flowers and snow green grass. I can go out without clothes, naked in my shirt: my passion protects me from the iciest wind." [21] " When I see her, when I consider her eyes, her face, her complexion, I tremble with fear like a leaf in the wind; a child has more sense than I retain

[20] Les poésies lyriques du troubadour Arnaut de Mareuil (ed. Ronald C. Johnston, Paris, 1935), pp. 1-5.
[21] Bernard de Ventadour in Berry, Florilège des troubadours, p. 177.

in the violence of my transports." [22] The true lover
never slept, but tossed and turned in his bed. His
thoughts were so centered on his lady that nothing else
interested him. But the effects of love were not purely
emotional and physical—it improved a man in every
way. " Behold again the good things which love gives:
it makes a vile creature into a distinguished man, a fool
into a man of agreeable conversation, a miser into a
spendthrift, and it transforms a rascal into a man of
honor. By it insane men become sages, the gauche
become polished and the haughty are changed into
gentle and humble men." [23] " For the ladies always
make valiant the most cowardly and the wickedest
felons: for however free and gracious a man is, if he did
not love a lady, he would be disagreeable to everyone." [24]
To this let us add a sentence from Pons de Chapteuil's
lament for his dead lady " The most valiant counts,
dukes, and barons were more *preux* because of her." [25]
The term *preux* implied the possession of the chief
virtue of feudal chivalry and was the most honorable
appellation that could be applied to a knight. Thus in
Pons' opinion the chivalric qualities were strengthened
by the worship of a lady. A man would be a better
knight if he loved—in fact it was doubtful whether a
man who did not adore a lady could be a true knight.

By developing this idea that a noble could not be a
perfect knight unless he loved a lady the troubadours

[22] *Ibid.*, p. 159.
[23] Aimeric de Pégulhan in Anglade, *Anthologie des troubadours*, p.
140.
[24] *Les chansons de Guilhem de Cabestanh* (ed. Arthur Langfors, *Les
classiques français du moyen âge*, Paris, 1924), p. 9.
[25] Alfred Jeanroy, *Anthologie des troubadours* (Paris, 1927), p. 44.

laid the foundation of courtly chivalry. If the doctrine was accepted by the noblemen, it would be bound to elevate woman's position in society. Although she could not fight herself, she could make men more *preux*. The troubadours did not, however, carry this theory to its logical conclusion—that a good knight should possess qualities pleasing to ladies. The ladies of troubadour poetry were passive goddesses who were adored whether they wished to be or not. Hence the troubadours laid little emphasis on the qualities which might make a lover acceptable. While it is true that the knight was expected to serve his adored one, this service consisted merely of fidelity and continuous worship. In short troubadour love was not mutual. The knight loved. The lady might or might not reward him, but she apparently never felt any great passion. Only when sexual intercourse became an integral and necessary part of the conception of love did the knight who wished to perfect himself by being in love feel called upon to make himself attractive to ladies. This important step was the work of writers of northern France who took over the ideas of the troubadours and modified them to suit themselves and their patronesses.

The difference between the conceptions of love expounded by the writers of northern and southern France has been explained as the result of a more realistic turn of mind among the former. I am very much afraid that this is simply an attempt to read into the twelfth century D'Artagnan and the traditional characteristics of the Gascon. When one considers the highly realistic poems composed by such troubadours as the monk of Montaudon and Bertrand de Born and the fantasy that marked so large a part of the Arthurian literature, this theory becomes completely unconvincing. Then I am not too sure that the northern conception should be called the more realistic. If realism consists of an adjustment of ideas to the actual conditions of life, the troubadour ideas of love deserve that appellation. They could be treated with amused tolerance by husbands and priests, while those of the north were in direct opposition to traditional morality.

Be that as it may it seems likely that the divergence in this respect between the writers of the north and those of the south was the result of the nature of the sources from which the former drew many of their ideas. The troubadours may have been acquainted with the works of Ovid, but they certainly did not exploit them as enthusiastically as did their northern colleagues.[26] The chief twelfth-century propagator of the northern ideas of courtly love, Chrétien de Troyes, translated the *Ars amatoria* and other Ovidiana.[27] By the middle of the twelfth century Ovid's work was recognized as the gospel of love, the chosen reading matter of Venus. It formed the basis for a large part of the contemporary handbook on the subject, the *De amore* of Andrew the Chaplain.

There can be little doubt that these writers who used Ovid as the source of all knowledge about love misunderstood his work. Ovid wrote in an intellectual and social environment completely unlike that of the twelfth

[26] Jeanroy has amply demonstrated the absence of classical influences in troubadour poetry. *La poésie lyrique des troubadours*, I, 64-68.

[27] Gustave Cohen, *Chrétien de Troyes et son oeuvre* (Paris, 1931), p. 84. Edmond Faral, *Recherches sur les sources latines des contes et romans courtois de moyen âge* (Paris, 1913).

century. Unfortunately we ourselves cannot be sure that we understand Ovid so accurately that we can measure the extent to which the mediaeval writers misused his work. Was Ovid writing a serious textbook on seduction or a comic piece which might have been entitled " See what trouble men will take for wenches? " But whatever may have been his exact object it is clear that Ovid was not writing of courtly love. His love was practical and sensual—it brought fun but not virtue. The Middle Ages accepted his maxims and either failed to comprehend or intentionally ignored the tenor of his work. Only when the difference between his conception and theirs became inescapable did they notice the divergence. For instance Ovid has much to say of the advantages of elderly women as mistresses and suggests that the seduction of a lady's maid is a sound method of starting a campaign against her virtue. A thirteenth-century translator of the *Ars amatoria* found these ideas absolutely unacceptable—they were clearly neither romantic nor courtly.[28] On the whole, however, Ovid was accepted as the canon of the laws of love. This alone seems sufficient to explain the nature of the conception of love held by these writers. In whatever way one may interpret Ovid's purpose, one thing seems absolutely certain—love to him meant sexual intercourse not mere admiration of a lovely and virtuous lady. This fact seems to have been recognized by some mediaeval writers. In one of the tales of Marie de France a jealous husband had decorated his wife's bower with mural paintings. In the center was Venus, goddess of love. On one side

[28] *La clef d'amors* (ed. Auguste Doutrepont, *Bibliotheca normannica,* V, Halle, 1890), lines 653-672, 1957-1970.

of her was a scene showing how men should " hold love and serve it legally and well," presumably as faithful husbands or strictly platonic lovers. On the other side of the goddess Ovid's *Ars amatoria* was being consigned to the flames.[29] Some two centuries later, Christine de Pisan, an enthusiastic admirer of courtly love on the troubadour model, warned her son to avoid reading Ovid if he wished to live chastely.[30]

The chief source of information about the ideas concerning love which were current in northern France in the second half of the twelfth century is Andrew the Chaplain's *De amore*.[31] Andrew's purpose was to write a comprehensive treatise on the subject. He discussed at length the conception of love that was in fashion among the romance writers of his day, the courtly love of Chrétien de Troyes. He mentioned with gentle irony the idea of platonic love. The numerous practical considerations which could be advanced in favor of traditional feudal morality were expounded. Finally the attitude of the church was fully explained and buttressed with solid arguments. As became a dispassionate critic Andrew tried to favor whichever conception he was discussing at the moment, but he could not entirely conceal the essential conservatism of his own views. Only when he was arguing for the traditional customs of the feudal world and the church was his heart fully in his work. His most spirited writing appears in the sec-

[29] *Guigemar* in *Die Lais der Marie de France* (ed. Karl Warnke, Halle, 1925), lines 233-244.

[30] Christine de Pisan, *Oeuvres poétique* (ed. M. Roy, Société des anciens textes français, Paris, 1886-1896), III, 39.

[31] *Andreae capellani regii Francorum de amore libri tres* (ed. E. Trojel, Kopenhagen, 1892).

tion entitled "*De reprobatione amoris*" which consists
largely of a furious diatribe against women in general.

The wide variety of opinions which found a place in
Andrew's work makes it a very difficult book to use.
One must carefully weigh every statement to discover
what his point of view was in that particular passage.
Besides it seems highly probable that Andrew was not
always entirely serious. Courtly love was a pleasant fad
that need not be taken too seriously. For instance in one
of his dialogues a man and a woman were discussing the
advisability of having unmarried girls practice love. The
woman pointed out that love as generally conceived was
bad for virgins. The man admitted that ordinary or
mixed love would injure their status, but pure love was
a very different matter. "This moreover [pure love]
consists in mental contemplation and affection of hearts;
it proceeds to a kiss on the mouth, to many embraces,
and to touching the nude private parts of the loved one,
but never to the extreme solace. . . . By such love no
virgin was ever corrupted nor did any widow or wife
suffer harm or loss of reputation." [32] In another dialogue
the man was attempting to persuade the lady that she
could not love her husband. He coolly fortified his case
by using or rather misusing one of the favorite precepts
of the ecclesiastical writers. "For as the apostolic book
teaches a vehement lover of his own wife is judged an
adulterer." [33] Hence the chief authority on which the
church relied for its command that husband and wife
have relations only in order to produce children was
used to make an argument for extra-marital relations.

[32] *De amore*, pp. 182-3.
[33] *Ibid.*, p. 147.

Later in his work Andrew used this same authority as it should be. These two instances are enough to convince me that Andrew was at times laughing merrily at his own work, and that the student of chivalry would do well to smile when he smiles.

Despite its peculiarities one can find in Andrew's book a comprehensive account of the ideas of courtly love which were current in his day. His first step was to make clear what he meant by love. " Love is a passion which comes from looking at and thinking too much about the body of one of the other sex as a result of which each one wishes above all else to be able to embrace the other and to fulfill the commands of love in the other's arms according to their mutual desire." [34] He is still more explicit in a later section entitled " what persons are fit for love." There he insisted that only those able to " perform the works of Venus " could be lovers.[35] From these two passages it seems evident that sexual intercourse was a necessary feature of love in Andrew's mind. This love was essential to men and women who wished to be worthy. " Nothing in the world is done that is good and courtly unless it springs from the fountain of love. Love is the origin and cause of all good . . . No man can do good deeds unless he is compelled by the persuasion of love." [36] " O, what a marvelous thing is love which makes a man shine with so many virtues and teaches him to abound with good moral customs." [37] According to Andrew love encourages chastity, for he who truly loves a lady has no

[34] Ibid., p. 3.   [36] Ibid., pp. 28-29.
[35] Ibid., p. 11.   [37] Ibid., p. 10.

interest in other women.[38] This all-powerful force for
good grows out of the good qualities of the participants.
A lady who is merely beautiful can always find lovers,
but if she lacks other virtues the lovers will be men of
little worth. Probity and wisdom are the qualities a
lover should seek in his mistress. The same general
virtues are to be sought in the masculine partner. While
it is pleasant to have a handsome lover, the more solid
qualities are of greater importance. The man should
have virtuous habits and a good reputation. He should
be noted for all the qualities that make a good knight.
Furthermore he should be neither too old nor too young
to make love effectively. On the other hand too lusty
a man is undesirable as he will find it impossible to be
faithful to any one lady and will demand from his mistress more than she is willing to give. This emphasis
on the mutuality of love is typical of Andrew's thought
and is the essence of his divergence from the troubadour
conception. Love is necessary to both men and women
and springs from the good qualities of each participant.
This idea had an important influence on the conception
of the perfect courtly knight. The troubadours were
satisfied if the knight adored a lady, but Andrew insisted
that he have the qualities required to win the lady's love.

Andrew the Chaplain's exposition of courtly love in
some ways accepted and in others defied the traditional
ideas of the feudal caste. Love was an emotion which
was confined to the noble class. While he admitted that
it was virtue rather than high birth that made a man or
woman lovable, he clearly believed it highly improbable
that the necessary virtues would appear in one of mean

[38] *Ibid.*

birth.[39] In another passage he was even more explicit. If a man should desire a peasant woman so strongly that he could not resist the temptation, let him rape her on the spot. A courteous approach would be wasted on a woman who could not possibly feel love.[40] But while he was able to adjust his conception of love to the aristo-cratic exclusiveness of the noble class, Andrew was unable to make it fit their ideas on matrimony. Being convinced that sexual relations were the essence of love he was clearly faced with two alternatives. He could preach marriage for love and love in marriage or he could defy all convention and insist on extra-marital love. It is evident that Andrew himself could see no good reason for avoiding the former course. In his dialogues several characters argued that married love was perfectly satisfactory, and Andrew developed their reasons with a skill and thoroughness that seems to me to indicate approval.[41] He was forced, however, to bow to the views of his noble patronesses. This love they were interested in was a new and wonderful thing and should not be confused with the political and procreative alliance that was feudal marriage. Hence Andrew in-sisted in general that love and marriage were incom-patible. His chief argument was based on his idea of the mutual nature of love. True love had to be freely given with no sort of compulsion. Husband and wife were bound to intercourse by their marriage vows—this could not be reconciled with love. His most important

---

[39] This question is discussed at length in several dialogues especially those entitled " *Loquitur plebeius nobili* " and " *Loquitur plebeius no-biliori feminae.*" *De amore*, pp. 36-69.

[40] *Ibid.*, pp. 235-6.

[41] *Ibid.*, pp. 141-155, 171-172.

subsidiary argument was much more artificial. True lovers were extremely jealous of one another. But jealousy was based on fear that the other partner would be unfaithful. As it was sinful for a husband and wife to suspect each other of infidelity, they could not be jealous and hence could not love. This reason is most unconvincing and entirely unworthy of Andrew's skill.[42] He could think of only one real argument against love in marriage and was forced to bolster his case as best he could. Thus, rather against his will, Andrew preached an utterly revolutionary doctrine. Men and women who wished to be worthy had to love, and love was adultery or at least fornication. This clearly troubled Andrew's conscience. Besides having various characters in his dialogues argue against these dangerous ideas he devoted the latter section of his book to tearing down the courtly doctrine which he had built up. There he preached chastity and fidelity to the marriage bond.[43] But as this section was frankly an attack upon love in all its forms, it did not solve his difficulty. Courtly love emerges from the pages of the *De amore* an extra-marital relationship in open defiance of feudal custom and ecclesiastical precept.

The *De amore* was apparently a popular work and was much used by later writers. Signs of its influence have been traced in French poets of the second half of the thirteenth century. Certainly that century saw the production of at least two French versions of Andrew's book. During the fourteenth and fifteenth centuries it was translated into Italian and German.[44] It seems im-

---

[42] *Ibid.*, pp. 141-155.   [43] *Ibid.*, pp. 313-361.
[44] See Trojel's introduction to *De amore*, pp. xv-xx.

probable, however, that during the first century after its composition it could have been anything more than a handbook for authors who wished to write about courtly love. Dashing young knights and lovely gay ladies did not pass their leisure reading latin treatises even when love was the subject. The *De amore* clearly owes its fame to the fact that it was a perfect source for contemporary writers, and it is even more valuable to the modern student. Andrew discussed every phase of his subject backwards and forwards. All the problems that troubled later writers were dealt with by him. When one has read his work one has a comprehensive idea of the doctrines of courtly love and a clear indication of how they would be viewed by nobleman and churchman.

The ideas which were expounded in a latin treatise by Andrew the Chaplain were popularized by a number of the contemporary writers of courtly romances of whom the most important was Chrétien de Troyes. Chrétien might be called with justice the official propagandist for the most influential patroness of courtly love, Marie, wife of Henry the Liberal, count of Champagne. Marie was the eldest daughter of Eleanor, duchess of Aquitaine, by her first husband, King Louis VII of France. Eleanor was the granddaughter of the earliest known troubadour, William IX, duke of Aquitaine, and her vast duchy embraced about half of the land of the *langue d'oc*. While she was queen of France and during the early years of her marriage to Henry Plantagenet, duke of Normandy, count of Anjou, and king of England, she was the foremost patroness of courtly poets. Eleanor is generally credited with the introduction of the troubadour ideas into northern France. When in the year 1173 Eleanor supported the rebellion against her husband which was led by their eldest son, she was imprisoned in Winchester castle where she spent most of her time during the remainder of Henry's life. Her place as chief patroness of courtly love was taken by her daughter, Marie. The latter's husband, Count Henry of Champagne, was the head of the most powerful feudal house in France. One of his brothers was count of Blois and Chartres, another count of Sancerre, and a third archbishop of Rheims. His sister was the third wife of King Louis VII. His county of Champagne was fertile and comparatively well organized politically. It contained flourishing towns, and was the site of the famous fairs of Champagne. Count Henry himself was noted for his knightly qualities and his keen interest in chivalric sports. In short Marie had great prestige, immense wealth, and a husband who was likely to tolerate courtly ideas. Thus it was no wonder that her court became the center for those who were interested in the new theories about love. It is very probable that Andrew the Chaplain had a place in her household, and it is certain that Chrétien de Troyes did. Andrew quoted Marie as the authority for a number of his statements about love, and Chrétien expressly stated that he wrote his *Chevalier de la charrette* at her request from material furnished by her.

The earliest surviving work of Chrétien de Troyes is a romance called *Erec et Enid*.[45] Its basic plot is extremely simple. Erec, the son of a Breton king, went

---

[45] Chrétien himself listed *Erec et Enid* as his first work. This is accepted by Voretzsch, *Introduction to old French literature*, pp. 277-8. Cohen places it after the translations from Ovid, but his reasons seem to me insufficient. *Chrétien de Troyes*, pp. 86-7.

forth to seek adventure. One night he was entertained
at the home of a poor vavassor who had a lovely and
charming daughter. Erec was greatly taken with the girl
and asked for her hand. When the father learned that
Erec was a king's son, he gladly gave his consent. Erec
brought Enid home to his father's court. Unfortunately
he was so deeply in love with her that he neglected
everything else and his reputation for prowess in
knightly sports began to decline. He decided to remedy
this by leaving Enid at home and going out adventuring
to win fresh fame as a knight. But Enid begged to be
taken along—she would be no trouble. During the rest
of the story Erec wandered over the face of the earth
with Enid riding dutifully behind him and being
savagely snapped at whenever she intruded herself on
his attention. Their adventures were the familiar ones
which always befell the knights of Arthurian romances.
Eventually Erec regained his reputation for prowess and
forgave Enid for having temporarily diverted him from
his career. They lived happily ever after. While there
was little that was essentially courtly about this tale,
there was enough to show that the new ideas of love
were in Chrétien's mind. Erec wanted to marry Enid
because of her beauty and charm,—that is for love.[46] He
became so absorbed in this love that he neglected his
duties as a knight. " Erec loved so much that no more
did he care for arms and went no more to tourneys. He
did not occupy himself with jousting: he made love to
his wife. Of her he had made his mistress; all his heart
and all his care he put into kissing and embracing her

[46] Christian von Troyes, *Erec und Enide* (ed. Wendelin Foerster,
Halle, 1890).

without taking pleasure in anything else. Often it was afternoon before he got up from beside her." [47] It is clear that when he wrote *Erec et Enid* Chrétien was familiar with the ideas of courtly love, but had his doubts as to how beneficial love was for a knight.

The next romance of Chrétien's which has been preserved was in many ways his most interesting work, *Cligès*. Since he wrote the *Erec et Enid* he had translated Ovid's *Ars amatoria* and had become more and more interested in love and its problems. He had even written a work about King Marc and Iseut the blond. Whether or not his lost work dealt with the love of Tristan and Iseut, it made him interested in the Tristan story. [48] He was apparently particularly fascinated by the chief question dealt with in this famous tale—what was the proper course of conduct when a man fell in love with another man's wife. If he turned away and renounced her, he injured love. If they carried on illicit relations, they committed adultery of which Chrétien clearly disapproved. In writing his *Cligès* Chrétien tried to give expression to all his new interests. The first part of the book was taken up by the courtship of Cligès' parents, Alexander and Soredamors. As the passages which I have quoted from it show this was a typical courtly romance which might be called unconventional only in that it ended in marriage. Then in the story of Cligès himself Chrétien set out to solve Tristan's problem. Cligès fell in love with Fenice who was affianced to his uncle, and she returned his affection. Here was the situation which had faced Tristan and Iseut, but

[47] *Ibid.*, lines 2434-2447.
[48] Cohen, *Chrétien de Troyes*, pp. 110-114

Chrétien knew a solution. Fenice had a nurse who possessed skill in magic. She would brew a potion for her
lady's husband which would render him impotent while
he was awake, but as soon as he fell asleep he would
dream that he enjoyed his wife and would awake perfectly satisfied. Thus Fenice retained her virginity.
Eventually she and Cligès grew tired of leaving their
love unappeased. The nurse then prepared a potion that
would make Fenice appear to be dead. Fenice drank it,
was buried, and spirited from the tomb by Cligès.[49] The
modern reader cannot feel that Chrétien has quite solved
the problem, but it was an interesting attempt. One
can easily see why the book as a whole should have
appealed to the devotees of courtly love. Besides the
account of the courtship of Alexander and Soredamors
and the extended discussion of a problem of interest to
all lovers, it contained long passages written in the
jargon of courtly love and expressing its ideas. Except
for his hesitancy about allowing his heroine to grant
her favors to two men, Chrétien wrote a romance in full
accord with the ideas expounded by Andrew the
Chaplain.

It was probably soon after the completion of *Cligès*
that Chrétien commenced the tale that was to be the
perfect romance of courtly love, the *Chevalier de la
charette*. This work is so extremely important to the
student of courtly chivalry that it seems necessary to
present a fairly extensive summary of it. Lancelot, the
best knight of Arthur's court, was in love with the
queen, Guinevere. One day as the court was disporting
itself in the forest, Lancelot learned that a wicked knight

[49] Christian von Troyes, *Cligès* (ed. Wendelin Foerster, Halle, 1884).

had abducted the queen. Starting in pursuit his horse
fell and was put out of commission. Just at that moment
a peasant came by driving a hangman's cart in which
criminals were carried to execution. Lancelot asked him
if he knew which way the queen had been taken. He
replied by inviting the knight to get into the cart.
Obviously a nobleman could undergo no greater humili-
ation than to be seen riding in such a cart. Lancelot
hesitated a moment, but then his love won and he
climbed into the cart. He then went through an
amazing series of adventures, all designed by Chrétien
to prove the force of his love. Late one afternoon as he
was wondering where he might find supper and shelter
for the night, he met a beautiful lady. She expressed
her willingness to extend hospitality to him if he would
sleep with her. Being very hungry Lancelot agreed, but
when the time came to retire he went to bed in his
shirt. As mediaeval men and women always slept naked,
to wear a shirt when going to bed with a lady was a sign
of chaste intentions. The girl was soon convinced that
Lancelot's love for Guinevere was too strong to allow
him to think of other women, and she got up and went
off to another room. A few moments later the scantily
clad and completely unarmed Lancelot was obliged to
rescue the lady from a group of armed ruffians whose
presence in her room was only vaguely explained by
Chrétien. Lancelot went on his way toward the country
where the queen was held captive. There is no point in
mentioning all the barriers he surmounted. The most
formidable was a bridge the footpath of which was the
edge of a sword. Lancelot took off his shoes and crossed,
but he was severely wounded in his hands and feet.

Eventually he reached the castle where the queen was held and challenged the wicked knight to combat. They fought in the courtyard while Guinevere and her ladies watched from the castle windows. At first Lancelot was almost helpless. He stood with his back to the queen's window, and so furious was his love that he could not resist turning his head to look at her instead of watching his foe. Finally one of the queen's ladies called out to him to get on the other side of the enemy so that he could watch the queen and fight too. Then, of course, he won quickly, so greatly did the sight of his lady increase his prowess. The wicked knight was beaten and the queen rescued. But Guinevere would not speak to her lover. She had heard, one must not ask how in an Arthurian tale, that Lancelot had hesitated before getting into the cart. That showed a flaw in his love. Another series of adventures was required before she forgave him, far too enthusiastically for her reputation. The story went on and on but we need follow it no further. Chrétien himself got sick of it and let someone else finish the work. Only one later incident is pertinent to our purpose. After the queen's return to Arthur's court, a great tourney was held. Lancelot entered in disguise and carried everything before him. The queen guessed who he was and sent him a note commanding him to fight as feebly as possible. Lancelot promptly allowed himself to be beaten about the field and driven off in disgrace. Next day he fought equally badly until the queen sent him word to do his best. Then no one could stand against him.[50]

[50] Christian von Troyes, *Der Karrenritter* (ed. Wendelin Foerster, Halle, 1899).

The *Chevalier de la charette* presented the doctrines
of courtly love in their most extreme form. It taught that
no obligation however sacred should stand in the way of
love. One of the basic tenets of feudal custom demanded
that a vassal should respect and if necessary defend with
his life the chastity of his lord's wife. Although loyalty
to one's obligations as a vassal was a fundamental virtue
of feudal chivalry, Lancelot, the perfect courtly knight,
committed adultery with his lord's wife. A knight particularly cherished his reputation for prowess in battle
and tourney. Lancelot almost allowed himself to be
overcome by the wicked knight because he could not
stop looking at his lady. On another occasion at the
queen's command he became the laughing-stock of a
tournament. A knight valued greatly his place in the
estimation of his contemporaries, his *prix*, but Lancelot
after a moment's hesitation rode in the hangman's cart
and became an object of derision to the whole countryside. Love was supreme. The perfect courtly knight
would abandon at its command everything that the
ordinary nobleman held dear. The mortal sin of adultery and the feudal crime of violating the wife of one's
lord were justified if required by love. No wonder the
essentially conservative Chrétien de Troyes hesitated to
write this romance and was careful to explain that the
plot had been supplied and its general treatment dictated
to him by his patroness, the Countess Marie of
Champagne.

Chrétien de Troyes and Andrew the Chaplain were
sophisticated men who looked at courtly love from a
rather detached point of view. They expounded its ideas
and pointed out the problems which were involved in

any attempt to apply them to actual life. Chrétien's romances, charming as they were, had a distinctly didactic tone. When the queen discovered the love between Alexander and Soredamor, she explained to them carefully the advantages of getting married instead of satisfying their desires illicitly.[51] Fenice, faced with the necessity of marrying the man she did not love, considered at length all possible courses.[52] Chrétien's characters were fully aware of their problems and discussed them in detail for the benefit of the reader. While the student of courtly ideas owes Chrétien a debt of gratitude for this characteristic of his work, it is refreshing to be able to turn for a moment to a twelfth-century writer who neither doubted nor worried. Marie de France accepted the doctrines of courtly love as a matter of course, and wove them deftly into her tales. Her conception of love was simple—it was physical attraction exerted by youth and beauty. The niece of his lady told Guigemar "This love is most proper—you are both beautiful."[53] Marie preferred to have her lovers find their solace in marriage, but if love and matrimonial obligations were in conflict, love always won. In one of her tales this doctrine was accepted by a wife. When she saw how beautiful her husband's mistress was, she retired to a convent so that the lovers might marry.[54] It was axiomatic to Marie that a young wife could not love an elderly husband and would eventually be captivated and led astray by a young gallant.[55] If access to the lady was extremely difficult, Marie had no objection

---

[51] *Cligès*, lines 2302-2310.
[52] *Ibid.*, lines 3063-3216.
[53] *Guigemar*, lines 451-453.
[54] *Eliduc*, lines 1006-1144.
[55] *Guigemar*, lines 209-217.

to supplying the young man with a magic ship or turning him into a bird for the occasion.[56] The difficulties
of adjusting love to feudal conditions did not trouble her
in the slightest. In the *Lai du Fresne* a baron had a
beloved mistress who was a foundling of unknown
origin. His vassals insisted that he marry a noblewoman
who could bear him heirs. The two lovers simply bowed
to the inevitable. While the baron looked about for a
suitable wife, his mistress prepared the house to receive
her. As the wedding preparations progressed, all the
relatives of the fiancée expressed their admiration for
the beauty and the amiability of the mistress. Of course
at the last minute the mistress was proved to be the
fiancée's twin sister and hence a woman of noble birth.
The two lovers were married and an excellent husband
was found for the deserted fiancée.[57] This story was
typical of Marie's insouciance. She had settled her
heroine's love problem—that of the other sister did not
trouble her. Chrétien would surely have supplied the
baron with a younger brother or dear friend with whom
the fiancée was secretly in love. Marie's tales were the
most delightful literary productions of the twelfth century. Courtly love and tales with the Celtic aroma
blended together by her skilful hand have great charm
for the modern reader. But aside from their literary
value her *lais* are of decided interest to the student of
courtly love. In them he can see how certain ideas of
the cult had become deeply implanted in the mind of a
highly intelligent noblewoman of the day. As the hopes
and aspirations of women lay at the base of courtly love,

[56] *Ibid.*, lines 266-269. *Yonec*, lines 109-119.
[57] *Le Fraisne.*

it is important to have its ideas expressed by a woman even if she does it in a fragmentary and casual way.

By the close of the twelfth century the doctrines of courtly love had been thoroughly expounded and established as a popular literary theme. The next three hundred years saw no diminution in the interest which this subject aroused in writers and their audiences. Although lyric love poetry waxed and waned both in quantity and quality, it was produced continuously in the castles and towns of France from the days of Thibaut of Champagne to those of Charles of Orleans. Semi-realistic love stories like the *Cligès* of Chrétien de Troyes had their counterparts in such works as the *Castelain de Coucy* and Christine de Pisan's *Livre du duc des vrais amants*. The incredibly long descriptions of the feelings of two lovers which marked the twelfth-century *Aeneas* were outdone in the thirteenth-century *Amas et Ydoine*. Finally all the lore of courtly love was summed up in the monumental and immensely popular *Roman de la rose*.[58]

Despite the quantity and variety of mediaeval literature dealing with romantic love the conception of the ideal courtly knight followed a remarkably stable pattern. The qualities which were required of a perfect noble lover by the fifteenth-century *Cent ballades* were not a whit different from those demanded by the fourteenth-century *Clef d'amors*, and Lancelot or Cligès as described by Chrétien de Troyes would have filled either set of specifications.[59] A knight had to love a lady.

[58] For a discussion of courtly love as found in the French literature of the later Middle Ages see Kilgour, *The decline of chivalry as shown in the French literature of the late Middle Ages*, pp. 108-194.

[59] *La clef d'amors*, lines 290-315. Jean le seneschal *Les cent bal-*

According to the followers of the troubadour tradition this love could consist of worship from a distance or a strictly platonic personal affection, but most writers expected it to assume a more tangible form. If a nobleman was to be acceptable to a lady, he had to have the qualities which kindled love. The primary requisite was possession of the ordinary chivalric virtues of prowess and loyalty. The author of the *Clef d'amors* assures his readers that a coward will never win a beautiful lady.[60] In the *Cent ballades* the lover is enjoined to maintain his reputation for prowess. In time of war he must seek glory in mines and on scaling-ladders. When the land is at peace, he should joust and tourney or better yet seek a good war in some foreign country.[61] There was, it is true, some dissent from this view that a worthy lover must be an effective and hardy warrior. Some writers maintained that ladies should love clerks rather than knights as the latter were far too rough and uncouth.[62] In general, however, the basic feudal virtues of prowess and loyalty were accepted as qualities requisite for a courtly knight.

A lady wished her knight to have a military reputation that would do her honor, but she was far more intimately interested in his possession of the qualities appropriate to the boudoir. The courtly knight should be handsome, should keep his teeth and nails clean, should wear neat and rich clothes. He was expected to be gay, witty, and

lades (ed. Gaston Raynaud, *Société des anciens textes français*, Paris, 1905), pp. 9-15.

[60] *La clef d'amors*, line 316.

[61] *Les cent ballades*, pp. 14-15.

[62] *Les débats du clerc et du chevalier* (ed. Charles Oulmont, Paris, 1911).

amusing. He must be courteous to everyone. He should be careful not to quarrel or brawl in the presence of ladies. The noble's fierce arrogance and proclivity for boasting must be curbed if he wished to arouse his lady's love. Above all the courtly knight must be able and willing to please the feminine taste. Perhaps few noblemen could compose songs in honor of their ladies, but they could at least learn to sing those written by others and to accompany themselves on a musical instrument. They could also master the intricate patter of courtly love and be prepared to take part in the endless debates which delighted its devotees. In short the ladies expected their lovers to be both warrior and *cavaliere servente*. In one of his *jeux-partis* the trouvère Perrot de Beaumarchais asked a lady whether she preferred a good knight full of prowess but lacking courteous qualities or a handsome blond youth who was good company and a master of the lover's art. The lady unhesitatingly chose the man of prowess. He could learn courtesy in her arms.[63]

When the courtly knight had won his lady's affection, he was expected to demonstrate his love by serving her. The troubadours thought it sufficient if he was loyal and composed songs in her honor, but later writers were more exacting. In the fanciful romances like those of the Arthurian cycle the knights served their ladies by killing dragons and subduing bandits whose castles were always filled with lovely captive maidens. The more realistic tales simply demanded that the lover honor his lady by performing deeds of prowess. The castellan of

[63] *Recueil général des jeux-partis français* (ed. Arthur Långfors, Société des anciens textes français, Paris, 1926), II, 175-177.

Coucy bore his lady's badge into as many tournaments as possible. The courtly knight must not only serve his lady but he must also be scrupulously careful of her honor. He must keep his love a close secret lest the lady's fame should suffer. Obviously even in the literature this was usually pure pretense. The ladies gloried in the knights who served them and had no desire to hide their love except perhaps from their husbands. The most that this injunction to secrecy meant was that a lover who had enjoyed his lady's favors should be discreet about his success. Finally the true knight would respect all ladies and defend their fame. Many a hero of courtly romance was characterized as one who would never listen to evil about ladies and would chastise anyone who defamed them. Such in brief was the conception of the qualities and behavior suitable to a courtly knight as it was expressed in contemporary literature.

It is easy to speculate about the possible effects of the propaganda for courtly love on the ethical conceptions of the noblemen of France, but very difficult to support conjecture with concrete evidence. Unfortunately few writers represent the point of view of the nobleman, and hence it is almost impossible to learn what his opinions were. As far as the glorification of adultery and the granting of a dominant place to women are concerned the scanty sources are unanimous. Although the biographer of William Marshal was familiar with courtly ideas and took care to emphasize his hero's ability to please ladies by dancing and singing, he was extremely indignant about a rumor that William was the lover of his lord's wife. William's own wife was mentioned at the time of her marriage to him, at his death, and once when she achieved temporary importance by being pregnant in a time of danger. If the Marshal served a lady, his biographer neglected to mention it. In the thirteenth century Philip de Novarre expressed opinions on this subject that would have satisfied any eleventh-century baron. One passage will suffice to show his attitude toward women. "Women have a great advantage in one way: if they wish to be held good, they can easily maintain this reputation by a single virtue. . . . If a woman is a *prode fame de son cors,* all her faults are hidden and she can go anywhere with high head." [64] To Philip submissiveness, chastity, and fertility were the only qualities of importance in a woman.

The attitude of a nobleman toward the doctrine of courtly love was expressed most fully in the book of advice which Geoffrey de la Tour Landry composed in the second half of the fourteenth century for the instruction of his young daughters.[65] La Tour Landry was familiar with courtly love and devoted some thought to the subject. He rejected without hesitation the more extreme precepts of the cult. Accepting fully the feudal and ecclesiastical attitude toward adultery he had nothing but condemnation for any woman who slipped from the path of strict virtue. He was careful to point out to his daughters that if a woman once lost her reputation for chastity, she was scorned by all worthy people. In fact La Tour Landry bemoaned the fact that such excellent ancient customs as burying illicit lovers alive

[64] Philippe de Navarre, *Les quatre ages de l'homme,* p. 20.
[65] *The book of the knight of La Tour Landry* (ed. and trans. G. S. Taylor, London, 1930).

had fallen into disuse. The good knight was also convinced that woman should be kept in her place. One
of his illustrative anecdotes shows this clearly. There
was once a woman who loudly opposed her husband in
public. When he tried to reprove her, she grew more
violent.

> And he, that was angry of her governance, smote her with his
> fist down to the earth; and then with his foot he struck her in
> the visage and broke her nose, and all her life after she had her
> nose crooked the which shent and disfigured her visage after,
> that she might not for shame show her visage, it was so foul
> blemished. And this she had for her evil and great language
> that she was wont to say to her husband.[66]

Although the more extreme doctrines of courtly love
seem to have made little headway in feudal society, the
available evidence indicates that those ideas which were
less decidedly in conflict with traditional mores gradually gained wide acceptance throughout the noble
caste. The author of the *Histoire de Guillaume le
Maréchal* was very proud of William's ability to entertain ladies by dancing and singing. In his account of
the one tournament in which he mentioned the presence
of ladies as spectators he asserted that William fought
unusually well because their eyes were upon him.[67]
The Marshal's biographer was primarily interested in a
purely feudal type of chivalry, but he felt it necessary
to make his bow towards the ideas of courtly love. There
can be no doubt that the belief that it was becoming
for a knight to be able to amuse ladies was rapidly
gaining ground in northern France during the thirteenth

---

[66] *Ibid.*, p. 22.
[67] *Histoire de Guillaume le Maréchal*, I, lines 3424-3562.

century. The respectable number of nobles who composed courtly poetry would alone serve to indicate this trend. Raynaud's *Bibliographie des chansonniers français* includes some thirty men of knightly rank in the list of authors. The most important figure both in respect to the quality and quantity of his production was Thibaut, king of Navarre and count of Champagne, but the poets of the period included in their ranks such potent feudal personages as Charles, count of Anjou, John, duke of Brittany, Hugh de Lusignan, count of La Marche, Thibaut, count of Bar-le-duc, and John, count of Macon.[68] Thus it is clear that the composition of love poetry was a respected avocation among the nobles of France.

This enthusiasm for poetry dealing with love does not, however, prove that courtly ideas had received general acceptance among the nobles of the thirteenth century. Courtly love had its devotees and many of them were men of high feudal rank, but there was certainly an opposition. This fact is amply demonstrated by the continued popularity of the *chansons de geste*. Alongside of lyric poetry and courtly romance flourished this literary type which appealed to the conservative noble who had little interest in love. The slowness of the feudal caste to accept even the mildest doctrines of courtly love is further shown by the attitude of La Tour Landry who lived a full century after Count Thibaut of Champagne. La Tour Landry had heard it stated that if a young girl or a married woman permitted a nobleman to worship her and talk to her of love without the

---

[68] Gaston Raynaud, *Bibliographie des chansonniers français des XIIIᵉ et XIVᵉ siècles* (Paris, 1884), II, 231-246.

thought of giving him any reward beyond a kiss or a gentle embrace, it made the woman livelier and gayer and might spur the man to perform great deeds of valor. Such love was not sinful and it might be beneficial, though here the knight had his doubts. Although young men might talk about love inspiring prowess, he suspected that it was merely a pleasant conceit. But whatever might be the advantages of such innocent amorous play he wanted his daughters to have none of it. For one thing thoughts of love and lovers diverted women's minds from religion. Then they were dangerous, for kisses and embraces led easily to more intimate caresses. Most serious of all to his mind was the menace to a lady's reputation. The most innocent relations with a man might lead to gossip, and many a woman had lost her honor without committing any sin. The only safe course was to give no possible cause for scandal.[69] Even if a young man should wish to marry a girl, she should be careful not to appear forward. La Tour Landry's father had once sent him to look over a prospective fiancée, but he had refused to consider her because she had received him with too little reserve. She had actually asked him not to delay too long before coming to see her again.[70] The fact that La Tour Landry felt called upon to devote a fair-sized section of his book to this subject seems to me to indicate that the ideas which he opposed were widely accepted among his acquaintances,

[69] La Tour Landry's discussion of courtly love was in the form of a discussion between himself and his wife. It is, however, clear that this was a purely literary device and that the ideas put in the lady's mouth were those of La Tour Landry. *The book of the knight of La Tour Landry*, pp. 139-149.
[70] *Ibid.*, pp. 15-16.

but his own rejection of them shows the persistence of
the conservative point of view even in as courtly a
region as Anjou.

The ideas which so sorely troubled La Tour Landry
were fully accepted by the biographer of his contemporary, Marshal Boucicaut. Love increased a man's
ambition to perform deeds of arms. It removed fear
from his heart. Good habits, joy and courage were
products of love. He asserted that Boucicaut, moved
by these considerations, found a lovely and worthy lady
whom he entertained by dancing, singing and composing songs in her honor. Her inspiration made him
shine in many jousts and tourneys.[71] Froissart, the chief
chronicler of fourteenth century chivalry, took this conception of the beneficial effects of love as a matter of
course. In describing the thoughts of King Edward III
about the beautiful but obstinately virtuous countess of
Salisbury he said

"And also if he should be amorous it would be entirely good
for him, for his realm, and for all his knights and esquires,
for he would be more content, more gay, and more martial;
and he would hold more jousts, more tourneys, more feasts,
and more revels than he had before; and he would be more able
and more vigorous in his wars, more amiable and more trusting
toward his friends and harsher toward his foes."[72]

Froissart also took great delight in describing the courteous treatment accorded by French and English knights
to any ladies whom the fortunes of war had placed at
their mercy. When a nunnery was pillaged and the nuns
raped, he was careful to point out that it had been done

[71] *Le livre des faicts du Maréschal du Boucicaut*, pp. 220-22.
[72] *Chroniques de Froissart*, II, 346.

by Germans.[73] Other contemporary historians shared Froissart's point of view. The biographer of Duke Louis of Bourbon described with relish the duke's courteous behavior toward the captured duchess of Brittany.[74]

Scanty and dispersed as the evidence is it seems to me to justify the formation of certain general conclusions about the extent to which the ideas of courtly love were absorbed into the ethical conceptions of the noble class. Those doctrines which came into direct conflict with the traditional prejudices and the environment of the feudal male remained in the realm of romance. The nobleman was unwilling to risk the legitimacy of his sons by countenancing adultery and when he married he allowed more practical considerations than love to govern his choice of a wife. As long as the feudal aristocrat was both governor and soldier, he was far too occupied to permit thoughts of woman and her pleasure to dominate his mind. But the less radical precepts of courtly love met no such unbending opposition. The knights were willing to accept the desire to honor a lady as a plausible and honorable motive for fighting. They had no objection to admitting that love could improve a man's prowess. They could even be persuaded to believe that a knight should devote some attention to pleasing women and should treat them with comparative courtesy. These ideas were not suddenly accepted throughout the feudal caste, but they spread slowly and by the end of the fourteenth century were generally recognized as an integral part of noble ethics. The propaganda of courtly love had been at least par-

[73] *Ibid.*, I, 171.
[74] *Chronique de Loys de Bourbon*, p. 38.

tially successful. Woman had edged her way into the mind of the feudal male and had elevated and enlarged her place in society as he recognized it. No longer was she merely a child-bearer and lust satisfier—she was the inspirer of prowess.

A discussion of the extent to which the ideas of courtly love were translated into practice can be little more than a study of the development of courteous treatment of women. The question of fundamental interest—whether or not courtly ideas increased illicit relations between noblemen and noblewomen—is completely insoluble. There is no evidence whatever that has any real bearing on the problem. Obviously scattered examples prove nothing, and even here every case of moral turpitude which can be found after the appearance of courtly love can be matched with one from the earlier period. If one accepts as true the wildest contemporary stories about Eleanor of Aquitaine, she still stands forth as a model of delicate propriety compared with Bertrade de Montfort. One can merely speculate on the basis of probabilities, and the result has validity only for the speculator. I suspect that the ideas of courtly love had little effect on the number of wives led astray and maidens corrupted. It is true, of course, as La Tour Landry pointed out, that the essentially innocent practices of courtly love might furnish temptation and opportunity for sin. A knight could never be quite sure whether a gay young man was whispering courtly nothings to his daughter or seriously attempting to seduce her. The man who was a humble worshipper while a husband was home might take a different guise if he were away. The innocent embraces with which a virtuous lady rewarded her lover's devotion might arouse too much mutual enthusiasm. If one believes the evidence which indicates that a generally accepted method of demonstrating platonic affection was for the lovers to sleep together entirely naked, one can easily agree that the ordinary practices of courtly love might lead to occasional errors. But these dangerous and entrancing possibilities seem to me to be outweighed by counter influences. The doctrines of courtly love enveloped seduction in a maze of forms and ceremonies. Men and women who were imbued with its ideas were less likely than their ancestors to yield to sudden bursts of mutual lust. The lady of the eleventh century who sought to mitigate the tedium of domestic life faced a direct plunge into the abyss of adultery, but courtly love supplied her granddaughter with a long and winding primrose path that allowed her plenty of opportunities to turn around and retrace her steps. Thus I am inclined to believe that the effects which the ideas of courtly love had on actual morality counteracted each other. This is my guess—the reader is welcome to his or her own.

While I have no doubt whatever that the partial acceptance of the ideas of courtly love by the feudal male produced a marked improvement in his treatment of gentlewomen, the demonstration of this fact must be made largely by means of indirect evidence. Contemporary historians recorded only the most striking examples of knightly courtesy toward ladies. The *Chanson de la croisade contre les Albigeois* states that Count Simon de Montfort even in the fierce bitterness of his war against the heretics refused to harm or even to rob

ladies.[75] When the crusaders took Lavaur they hanged
the commander of the garrison and eighty of his knights
and burned four hundred inhabitants of humble birth.
The sister of the commander was thrown in a well and
covered with stones. But a crusading knight behaved
as a man who was *preux* and loyal—he arranged for the
escape of all the other women of gentle birth who had
been in the town.[76] A century and a half later similar
examples appeared in the chronicles of the Hundred
Years War. When the captured duchess of Brittany
was led before the duke of Bourbon, she asked if she
were a prisoner and received the reply " No, we do not
war on ladies." Except for a copy of a treaty between
the duke of Brittany and the king of England all the
lady's effects were returned to her and she was given
an escort to the nearest castle held by her partisans.
The duchess might well say that " God had done her
grace to be in the hands of such a knight " [77] When
Edward III occupied the castle of Pois, he found it
deserted except for two noble girls. The two maidens
would have been raped by the low-born archers had
not two noted knights, John Chandos and Reginald
Basset, rescued them *" pour la cause de gentilece."* [78]
On another occasion the French were besieging the
castle of Thun. The English commander had with him
as his mistress a renegade French nun of gentle birth.
The lady was pregnant and the tumult of the siege

---

[75] *La chanson de le croisade contre les Albigeois* (edited and translated by Paul Meyer, *Société de l'histoire de France*, Paris, 1875-1879),
II, 71.

[76] *Ibid.*, p. 89.

[77] *Chronique de Loys de Bourbon*, p. 38.

[78] *Chroniques de Froissart*, III, 387.

engines annoyed her. Hence the courteous besiegers allowed her to pass through their lines to take refuge in another fortress controlled by her lover.[79] Throughout Froissart's pages we find knights and squires patrolling the streets of captured towns to protect women of rank from the lust of the common soldiers. The testimony of the chronicles is the more credible because they occasionally record cases in which nobles failed to be courteous to ladies. Monstrelet tells how the noblemen who were in the French army which captured Soissons in 1414 joined the ordinary soldiers in indiscriminately raping women of all ranks.[80] But the fact that this incident profoundly shocked Monstrelet and other contemporary writers seems to indicate that such conduct on the part of nobles was rare.

Unfortunately examples of courteous behavior in time of war do not prove much about the ordinary relations between men and women. Chronicles rarely describe in detail courtships, seductions, or scenes from domestic life. One of the most striking exceptions, Froissart's account of Edward III's efforts to seduce the countess of Salisbury, seems to me more likely to be a product of courtly imagination than of actual knowledge.[81] A chronicler may stand on the field of battle, but he is rarely invited into the boudoir. The historian of private and domestic manners must rely almost exclusively on didactic works like that of La Tour Landry and on contemporary literature. This material is most useful in

---

[79] *Ibid.*, II, 214.

[80] *La chronique d'Enguerran de Monstrelet* (ed. L. Douet-D'Arcq, Société de l'histoire de France, Paris, 1859), III, 9-10.

[81] *Chroniques de Froissart*, II, 131-137.

establishing ideals of domestic behavior, but it is highly unreliable as evidence for actual practices. Nevertheless as no other material is available it seems worth while to present some generalizations based on literary sources. If the anecdotes of La Tour Landry are authentic, brutality to women was still common in the fourteenth century. Men beat their wives and foully berated ladies in public gatherings. On the other hand the literature as a whole seems to indicate a development of courtesy. Such comparatively realistic works as the *Castelain de Coucy* and *Le livre du duc des vrais amants* show women treated with a gentleness and consideration far removed from the brutality of the *chansons de geste*. The available material gives no ground for a stronger statement. There is, in reality, little positive evidence that the noblemen of the thirteenth, fourteenth, and fifteenth centuries treated ladies more courteously than had their predecessors of the eleventh. The change in ideas on the subject is clear cut and definite, but the modification of actual practices remains intangible.

While it seems impossible to discover to what extent the noblemen of mediaeval France put into practice the ideas of courtly love, it appears worth while to speculate as to what the results would have been had they done so to a reasonable degree. If any large number of knights followed the precepts which it is clear they accepted as ideals, it marked an important step in the development of the noble class. The warrior turned to devote a part of his time and attention to the arts of the boudoir. He learned to be reasonably neat and clean in dress. He acquired the habit of speaking gently and courteously to ladies. Above all he was forced to master some skills other than those used on the battlefield. He learned to sing, to dance, to play an instrument, and perhaps even to compose songs and dances. If he wished to attract ladies, he needed a ready wit and a mastery of the patter of courtly love. Thus the knight became of some use in a milieu other than that of a battle. The ability to please ladies could be turned without too much difficulty to pleasing princes. Although the trend of martial and political change gradually deprived the nobleman of his functions as governor and soldier, he remained a most amusing companion. Thus the training given the noble class by their acceptance of the doctrines of courtly love may have done much to prepare the knight to become a courtier and a gentleman.

V

CRITICISMS AND COMPROMISES

THE reader who has perused the last three chapters must realize that mediaeval France knew neither a single ideal of knighthood nor a universally accepted code of chivalry. The three types of chivalry were to some extent at least irreconcilable. Léon Gautier performed to his own satisfaction the rather astonishing feat of fitting *Raoul de Cambrai* and *Roland*, feudal and religious chivalry, into one pattern, but he was forced to consign *Lancelot* and the courtly ideal to the outer darkness. The fact that these three sets of chivalric ideas were mutually exclusive was fully realized during the Middle Ages. Churchmen and trouvères paused now and then in the midst of propagating their own theories to take a shot at those of their rivals, and knightly writers did not hesitate to criticize both the religious and the courtly ideals. But while the three sets of chivalric ideas were irreconcilable as a whole, one could easily choose elements from each to form a consistent composite ideal. When trouvères described the heroes of their tales or didactic writers propounded codes of conduct for young nobles, they constructed perfect knights to suit their own tastes. My object in this chapter is to glance at some of the criticisms which churchmen and protagonists of courtly love made of each other's theories and of those of feudal chivalry and then to examine some of the composite ideals which may be found in contemporary literature. In short I hope to demonstrate the essential irreconcilability of the three types of chivalry and to show how this difficulty was solved by the men of mediaeval France.

As one would expect, the largest volume of criticism of chivalric ideas and practices came from the pens of ecclesiastics. These traditional custodians of the truth considered it their privilege and even their duty to denounce their opponents while those who disagreed with them hesitated to incur the wrath of the church. The opinions of the churchmen about feudal and courtly chivalry were openly expressed and can easily be found by the historian, but the replies of the other side must be pieced together from sly, fugitive passages scattered through the mass of contemporary literature. Andrew the Chaplain placed his general assault on women and love in a separate section of his book under the title *De reprobatione amoris,* but his direct attacks on the moral teachings of the church were carefully tucked away in his imaginary colloquies. Not until the Renaissance did one dare to attack chastity openly. Hence when we examine the ecclesiastical views, we deal with fine, strong trumpet blasts, but the opposition can be heard only in soft defiant whistles.

In analyzing the ecclesiastical attitude toward feudal chivalry it is necessary to bear in mind that the precepts of the latter in the abstract did not conflict in any way with the teachings of the church. Prowess, loyalty, generosity, and the desire for glory could be admired by both churchmen and laymen. The divergence between the two points of view became apparent only when these virtues were concretely interpreted and translated into practice. The mediaeval church had no objection to just wars, but its definition of legitimate warfare if taken literally would have banned practically all contemporary military activities except the crusades. A war was just when it was conducted by a sovereign prince in defense of his patrimony or to suppress evil-doers. Even then the motive had to be the desire for justice not the hope of profit. In short if the teachings of the church had been strictly observed, there would have been little fighting during the Middle Ages. But war was the principal function of the feudal class, and the ability to fight well was the chief virtue of feudal chivalry. While both nobles and ecclesiastics admired prowess as a knightly quality, their respective attitudes toward the practice of that virtue differed widely.

Another circumstance which tended to conceal the true relation between feudal chivalry and Christian ethics was the church's inclination to compromise as much as possible with the political and economic conditions of the lay world. Although practically all mediaeval warfare was unjust according to the church's teaching, it was the traditional occupation of the dominant class of contemporary society. Hence churchmen usually forbore to attack war itself but instead denounced its concomitants—homicide and rapine. The ecclesiastical writers raised the desire for glory into a high place among Christian virtues while fulminating denunciations against those who sought what they chose to call vainglory. The anxiety of the church to adjust its teachings to its environment can be seen clearly in the *Summa theologica* of Thomas Aquinas, and it appears particularly strongly in his discussion of questions which were closely related to the precepts of feudal chivalry. Where sexual morality was involved as in courtly chivalry, the church was absolutely intransigent, but its treatment of the political and economic peccadillos of the feudal caste was highly sympathetic.

The most interesting phase of the church's attitude toward feudal chivalry was its pronouncements about the knightly enthusiasm for winning glory. In general as I have indicated above ecclesiastical writers were inclined to consider the desire for fame as a worthy motive As early as 1128 Galbert of Bruges mentioned it as one of the admirable traits of Charles the Good, count of Flanders. When Count Charles found that he had no foes who dared oppose him, he felt obliged to do something that would reflect honor on his fief and keep his knights in trim for war. So he took two hundred knights and made an expedition into Normandy and France where he tourneyed against the local lords. In this way he greatly increased "his own fame and the power and glory of his country." Whatever sin was involved in this proceeding Charles made amends for by generous alms giving.[1] In Galbert's mind for a nobleman to risk committing the sin of homicide for the sole purpose of winning glory was a sin but not a very serious one. When one considers that in 1130 the council of Clermont prohibited tournaments, it seems probable that Galbert viewed these military sports more leniently than most of his fellow churchmen.

[1] Galbert de Bruges, *Histoire du meurtre de Charles le Bon* (ed. H. Pirenne, *Collection de textes pour servir à l'étude et à l'enseignement de l'histoire*, Paris, 1891), p. 9.

Certainly Thomas Aquinas would have maintained that Count Charles had sought not glory but vainglory. To him glory was the object of magnanimity, one of the chief Christian virtues. The magnanimous man yearned for the honor and praise which could be won by performing great and difficult deeds. He always preferred a project promising glory to one holding hopes of profit. But if honor "which greatly excells among external things" was to be gained, both the act and its end had to be worthy. He who tried to draw glory from a deed which existed only in his imagination or which was essentially unworthy was a seeker for vainglory. A deed was unworthy if it was estimable only in the eyes of men but not of God or if its purpose was improper.[2] In short glory could be gained by performing arduous feats pleasing to the church and in accord with its teachings. The fame which came from all other activities admired by men or from skilful boasting was mere vainglory.

Ecclesiastical denunciations of the search for glory as it was conducted by most knights were numerous. In his *De laude novae militiae* St. Bernard of Clairvaux lists the "appetite for inane glory" with anger and greed as the motives which led the knights of his day into unworthy wars. The Templars were admonished to go into battle thinking about victory instead of glory.[3] A century later the famous preacher Jacques de Vitry stated that knights who took part in tournaments were guilty of the sin of pride because they sought " the praise

[2] Thomas Aquinas, *Summa theologica*, II, II, quaestio CXXIX, articuli 1-2; quaestio CXXXII, articuli 1-4.
[3] Migne, *Patrologia latina*, CLXXXII, 923, 926.

of men and inane glory." [4] Exactly the same idea was also expressed by Jacques' contemporary Caesarius of Heisterbach.[5] The other type of vainglory described by Aquinas, that which had its source in pure boasting, was colorfully and forcefully described by John of Salisbury under the heading " of braggart soldiers who are of no use for service."

The more boastful they are in the hall, the more certain it is that when it comes to the issue of an actual battle, they will send ahead their servants into the fight in droves . . . while they themselves, to save their skins, trail behind the rear guard. . . . But afterwards when they return home without a wound or a scratch (as generally happens), . . . each boasts that about his temples he narrowly missed a thousand deaths. Indeed never thereafter will you be able to endure the dazzle of their glory. A tale of this kind will be handed down to the hundredth year; their sons who will be born and grow up, will tell it over to their sons. If they break any lances, which their artful laziness has contrived to have made as fragile as hemp, if the gold leaf or red-lead or other coloring matter has been knocked off their shields by some chance blow or other accident, their garrulous tongue, if they find any to listen, will make the incident memorable from century to century.[6]

In short in respect to glory it seems clear that the ideas of the church differed radically from those held by most knights. The kind of glory sought by the nobles of mediaeval France was vainglory in the eyes of the church.

The discussion of ecclesiastical criticisms of feudal chivalry might well end here. Only in the case of glory did the teachings of the church definitely diverge from

    [4] *The exempla of Jacques de Vitry* (ed. T. F. Crane, *The Folk-Lore Society*, London, 1890), p. 63.
    [5] Caesarius of Heisterbach, *The dialogue on miracles*, I, 512.
    [6] Dickinson, pp. 184-5.

the ethical ideals avowed by the feudal class. But the church's denunciations of the knightly ways of practicing the chief virtue of feudal chivalry, prowess, were too persistent and too strong to be entirely neglected. I have already pointed out the essential impossibility of practicing prowess without running the risk of committing homicide. This practical divergence between religious and knightly ideas is best illustrated in the church's attitude toward tournaments. We have seen in a previous chapter that the tournament was the crucible in which the ideas of feudal chivalry took form and remained throughout the Middle Ages the very heart of chivalric practice. It is, of course, easy to understand why the church centered its attacks on these knightly sports. In the case of feudal war the question whether it was legitimate or not was always open to debate and too vigorous denunciations would only serve to annoy the princes who were engaged in it. But homicide committed in tournaments could never be justified under the teachings of the church—they were not fought to defend one's country nor to suppress evil-doers. Moreover in general these exercises were not popular with the feudal princes who considered them a waste of valuable man power and a potential cause of disorder.

As early as 1130 the council of Clermont prohibited tourneys as homicidal contests and refused burial in consecrated ground to anyone killed in them. This decree was confirmed by the Lateran councils of 1139 and 1179.[7] The ban on tournaments appeared in the canon law among the *Decretals* of Pope Gregory IX.[8]

---

[7] H. Leclerq, *Histoire des conciles*, V, I, 688, 729; II, 1102.
[8] *Decretalium Gregorii papae IX*, liber V, titulus XIII.

The thirteenth-century Dominican, Raymund de Peniafort, devoted a chapter of his *Summa de poenitentia* to
this subject. He pointed out that knights who were slain
in tournaments would be denied Christian burial and
that those who caused their death were clearly guilty
of homicide.[9] Bartholomaeus de Chaimis in his *Interrogatorium sive confessionale* directed priests who were
hearing the confessions of secular lords to inquire particularly whether they encouraged tourneys.[10] Jacques
de Vitry stated that seven mortal sins—pride, envy, hate,
avarice, extravagance, luxury, and homicide—were committed by those who frequented these martial games.
The pride was involved in the search for glory and the
envy in ill will toward those who gained honor. The
avarice appeared in the enthusiasm of the knights for
capturing prisoners, horses and arms. The sin of luxury
was committed by fighting to please the immodest
women who attended tournaments and by wearing their
favors in the fray.[11] Caesarius of Heisterbach found a
way to simplify the indictment against tourneys. In his
mind the contestants were guilty of pride because they
sought the praise of men and of disobedience for violating the commands of the church.[12]

Next to homicide the taking of booty was the knightly
practice most persistently denounced by the church.
Although in theory a knight fought for glory, plunder
was an integral part of mediaeval warfare, and the hope

[9] *Summa de poenitentia et matrimonio sancti Raymundi de Peniafort*
(Rome, 1603), p. 161.
[10] Bartholomaeus de Chaimis, *Interrogatorium sive confessionale*
(Regensburg, 1474).
[11] *The exempla of Jacques de Vitry*, pp. 62-64.
[12] Caesarius of Heisterbach, *The dialogue on miracles*, I, 512.

of capturing prisoners, horses, and arms was an important motive for tourneying. While it was undoubtedly possible to practice prowess without committing rapine, few knights could be expected to do so. Here again Thomas Aquinas gave as much consideration to the habits of the feudal class as the plain teachings of the church would permit. As the unjust had no right to property, it was proper to take booty in a legitimate war provided one's motive for fighting was to enforce justice rather than to seek profit. But since few mediaeval wars were legitimate according to St. Thomas' definition, this was not of much assistance to the knight who wished to supplement his income from the proceeds of battle and tourney.[13] When he plundered merchants or peasants, captured arms or horses, or collected ransoms for prisoners, he committed the sin of rapine. Moreover the church insisted that before receiving absolution for his offense, the knight had to prove his penitence by making restitution. William Marshal on his death bed maintained that this doctrine was unreasonable—if it were insisted on no knight could be saved.[14] Most nobles must have calmly ignored the requirement with at least the passive consent of the clergy. Nevertheless throughout the Middle Ages ecclesiastics wrote and preached against knightly rapine. Jacques de Vitry mentioned it as one of the sins committed by those who fought in tournaments.[15] The proponents of religious chivalry denied that a plunderer could be a true knight. In short some churchmen main-

[13] Thomas Aquinas, *Summa theologica*, II, II, quaestio XL, articulus I; quaestio LXVI, articulus 8.
[14] Painter, *William Marshal*, pp. 285-6.
[15] *The exempla of Jacques de Vitry*, p. 63.

tained that he who plundered was not really a knight while others simply denounced knightly plunderers. Both groups were equally opposed to a vital even if frequently disavowed practice of feudal chivalry.

In regard to the ideas of courtly chivalry the church was able to adopt a far more intransigent attitude than toward those of the feudal type. The latter presupposed perpetual warfare—the former perpetual adultery. But while war was hated by the church it could under certain conditions be justified under its teachings and it was the chief function of the dominant class in mediaeval society. Adultery on the other hand could never be justified in Christian ethics and was in opposition to the traditional mores and social needs of the feudal class. Unfortunately for the historian ecclesiastical writers could attack the bases of courtly love without honoring the cult with specific mention. Since the church had always denounced adultery and fornication, it need only continue to do so. As a result I can find only one orderly presentation of the church's objections to courtly love—the *De reprobatione amoris* of Andrew the Chaplain. Most of the criticisms which one can feel certain were made with courtly love in mind were aimed at the pleasant, merry, and essentially innocent practices between men and women which formed such an important part of its paraphernalia.

Andrew the Chaplain commenced his denunciation of courtly love by stating the basic fact that sexual intercourse outside of marriage was a mortal sin. " O poor, and insane, and more than worthy to be thought bestial is he who for momentary delight of the flesh relinquishes eternal joy and labors to commit himself to a perpetually flaming hell." He then went on to point out that the Bible commands one to love one's neighbor and that illicit love harms not only its recipient but others as well. Moreover love often leads to quarrels, war and homicide. The seduction of a wife, sister, or daughter frequently ends a close friendship. The true lover is so absorbed in his passion that he is its absolute slave and good for nothing else. Then the great expense of wooing a lady often leads a man to commit theft or robbery. Perjury and lieing were almost necessary adjuncts of illicit love. Occasionally too enthusiastic a lover might put away or even slay his wife, and jealous husbands sometimes cast off unfaithful spouses. Thus marriage which God had created could be destroyed by love. Finally love is harmful to a man's body. The very act of Venus decreases man's strength, and absorption in love spoils his appetite. He also loses sleep and much needed rest. As it is a sin to diminish the bodily powers given by God, love should be shunned. Andrew concluded by stating that intercourse shortened a man's life.[16] One wonders whether he meant to suggest that love was a slow and pleasant type of suicide.

The most precise and fluent critic of the courtly customs which were spreading through western Europe in the twelfth century was John of Salisbury. Some of his remarks were leveled at practices which seemed to him to indicate a softening of knightly hardihood and which may or may not have had a connection with courtly love. Others clearly referred to customs engendered by the new cult. In the former category belong his violent denunciations of the military qualities of the knights of his day.

[16] *De amore*, pp. 313-338.

. . . Our youth as if they were born but to consume the fruits of the earth, sleeping until daylight, postponing honorable duties to fornication, pursuing sensual pleasure the live-long day, are better acquainted with the cithern, the lyre, the tambourine and the note of the organ at the banquet, than with the sound of the clarion or trumpet in the camp. [17]

The gamester, the fowler, and, whereat you will the more greatly marvel, makers of foolish songs, and men who have never dealt in any manly deeds nor have the marks of duty on them (for bristling beard and hardened skin are now in disrepute as being unmeet for works of wantonness) today put on the soldier. . . .[18]

As men are always inclined to compare unfavorably the soldiers of their day with heroes of the past, these passages should not be taken too seriously. The references to musical instruments, foolish songs, and the knights' desire to please the ladies seems to me to show that John was criticizing the courteous practices preached by the proponents of courtly love. The reader may form his own opinion on the matter.

In other passages of the *Policraticus* John's remarks were clearly and precisely aimed at the customs of courtly love.

The singing of love songs in the presence of men of eminence was once considered in bad taste, but now it is considered praiseworthy for men of greater eminence to sing and play love songs which they themselves with greater propriety call *stulticinia,* follies.[19]

[17] Dickinson, p. 194.

[18] *Ibid.*, p. 226.

[19] *Frivolities of courtiers and footprints of philosophers, being a translation of the first, second, and third books and selections from the seventh and eighth books of the Policraticus of John of Salisbury* (translated by Joseph B. Pike, Minneapolis, 1938), p. 32.

Would that pastoral lays and lover's follies were silent in the home of the wise, and that those themes which benefit or charm without being base or demoralizing sounded in the ears of all! [20]

John objected to having knights learn the arts of being pleasing to ladies because he believed that it decreased their value as soldiers. As for love songs and *pastourelles* they were both frivolous and dangerous to sound morality. As John of Salisbury was the chief twelfth-century exponent of religious chivalry, his criticisms of the courtly type are particularly valuable. In his mind at least the two were definitely incompatible.

As I have suggested above it is almost impossible to find specific references to the practices of courtly love in mediaeval religious literature. Theologians and canonists vigorously denounced illicit sexual relations, but such relations can hardly be considered an invention of courtly lovers. Only in the handbooks for confessors did the ecclesiastical writers discuss the practices which they considered objectionable in sufficient detail to enable one to use their statements with confidence. Bartholomaeus de Chaimis directed confessors to ask men whether they " had made songs or sonnets or had sung, read, or heard with delight lascivious, turpitudinous, and dishonest words intended to provoke himself or others to lasciviousness." Bartholomaeus clearly disapproved of the love songs which formed so important a part of courtly love. Incidentally it is interesting to notice Bartholomaeus' attitude toward such pleasant amorous play as that permitted to " pure " lovers by Andrew the Chaplain. The confessor was to ask whether

[20] *Ibid.*, p. 323.

a man had kissed, embraced, or touched a woman with delight—if so he had committed a mortal sin.[21] This point of view was fully upheld by Thomas Aquinas. " The touch and the kiss . . . when they are libidinous, are counted among the mortal sins." [22] Thus even the gentlest and most harmless practices of courtly love were banned by the church. Between its teachings and the ideas of courtly chivalry no compromise was possible.

Although churchmen could pour forth their denunciations against the ideas and practices which they considered inimical to their doctrine, their opponents dared not reply in kind. The immense weight of traditional authority gave full license to ecclesiastics while imposing comparative silence on those who disagreed with them. This situation was not a serious burden for the proponents of feudal chivalry. As the chivalric ideals held by churchmen and knights diverged in interpretation and practice rather than in basic theory, the latter and the writers who expressed their ideas could simply go their way ignoring the church's views. But courtly chivalry fundamentally and definitely contravened the teachings of the church. Usually its exponents contented themselves with stating their ideas and allowing their readers to compare them with the ethics of Christianity. Occasionally, however, a daring writer ventured to tuck away in some fairly obscure corner of his work a direct attack on ecclesiastics and their doctrines. Others perhaps were moved to treat the ideas of the church with gentle irony.

Few scholarly pastimes are more dangerous than that

---

[21] Bartholomaeus de Chaimis, *Interrogatorium sive confessionale.*

[22] Thomas Aquinas, *Summa theologica*, II, II, quaestio CLIV, articulus 4.

of attempting to say when writers of an age long past were being ironical. Unless the irony was hopelessly bald and clumsy, it is impossible to prove its existence. Did Marie de France smile quietly as she made a wife retire to a nunnery in order to permit her husband to marry his beautiful mistress? This solution of the eternal triangle was so gloriously out of accord with ecclesiastical law that one is tempted to think that Marie was being mischievous, but it is perfectly possible that she was guilty of nothing more than innocent insouciance. Then Chrétien de Troyes, the most courtly of romancers, painted his virtuous hero, Perceval, as incredibly rude, ingenuous, and naive. Did he intend to depict simply the pure innocence of uncorrupted youth or did he mean to suggest that a chastely inclined knight was bound to be rather uncouth? These questions can never be answered—perhaps they should never have been raised. But it is important to remember that irony might be the explanation of some of the puzzling episodes in mediaeval literature and that it would have been a safe medium for opposition to ecclesiastical ideas.

The most thoroughgoing and skilfully expressed direct attack on the views of the church is found in a well known passage from *Aucassin et Nicolette*.

What have I to do with Paradise? I do not seek to enter there but only to have Nicolette, my very sweet friend whom I love so much. For into Paradise go none but the sort of people I will tell you of. There go the aged priest, the old cripple, and the maimed who all day and all night cough before the altars and in the ancient crypts; there go those who wear worn old mantles and old tattered clothes; who are naked, barefoot, and covered with sores; who are dying of hunger, thirst, cold, and misery. These people go to Paradise—with them I have nothing to do. But to Hell I will go, for to Hell go the fair clerks and the handsome knights who have been slain in tourneys and magnificently conducted wars; . . . there go the lovely courtly ladies who have two or three lovers besides their husbands; there go the gold, silver, and rare furs; there go the harpers, jongleurs, and the king of this world. With these will I go if only so that I may have with me Nicolette, my very sweet friend.[23]

Andrew the Chaplain expressed his criticism of the ecclesiastical attitude toward courtly love in a less direct fashion than did the author of *Aucassin et Nicolette*. Instead of presenting an indictment of the Christian heaven he chose to create one to suit his needs. When ladies who had followed the precepts of courtly love died, they were transported to a delectable spot where they sat magnificently dressed and surrounded by courteous knights under the spreading branches of a great tree which bore all known varieties of fruits. From the roots of the tree sprang fragrant fountains. While all kinds of musical instruments charmed the ears of the ladies and their knights, tumblers played and leaped for their further entertainment. The entire resources of this marvelous spot were dedicated to the pursuit of pleasure. But Andrew was not content merely to supply a heaven for the adherents of courtly love—he created two hells for its opponents. The light and voluptuous ladies who had granted their favors too freely were placed in a wet, humid place where they served the pleasure of an army of attending males. Finally the ladies who had refused to love, the chaste wives and virgin maidens, were condemned to a hot, dry region fully exposed to the burning

[23] *Aucassin et Nicolette* (ed. Mario Rogues, *Les classiques français du moyen âge*, Paris, 1925), p. 6.

rays of the sun. There they reposed on seats made of thorn-covered rods. A group of men assigned to the task kept the rods continually moving back and forth so that the ladies could feel the full effect of the thorns.[24]

Andrew the Chaplain's highly ingenious picture of the future life apparently did not meet with the approval of Drouart la Vache who translated the *De amore* into French verse. He omitted this section of the book, but summarized its contents in a sentence which seems to modify Andrew's meaning. " For by that God who does not lie and who formerly died for us those women who are in Paradise have scarcely more solace and joy than those have who in this life always served true love loyally." [25] The courtly ladies according to Drouart will not go to heaven, but they will have a residence almost equally pleasant. As for the ladies whom Andrew consigned to thorny seats, they must have been among the inhabitants of Drouart's heaven. In short Drouart la Vache did not criticize the ecclesiastical view—he simply tried to supply a secondary heaven for true lovers.

In all probability a thorough search through the courtly literature of mediaeval France would produce a fair number of sly and fugitive attacks on the church's teachings. I must content myself with one more sample—a brief passage from the *Roman de la rose ou de Guillaume de Dole*. The Emperor Conrad was holding a splendid fête. Early in the morning he sent the " jealous and envious " off into the forest to hunt accompanied by men who were ordered to see that they

[24] *De amore*, pp. 99-104.
[25] *Li livres d'amours de Drouart la Vache* (ed. Robert Bossuat, Paris, 1926), p. 82.

did not return too soon. This left the field clear for
the gay young knights and ladies. "They did not think
about their souls: they had neither bells nor churches,
nor other chaplains than the birds." [26]

Enough has been said, I believe, to show conclusively
that the three sets of chivalric ideas were too incompatible to be combined in any single ideal of knighthood that
would satisfy everyone. On the other hand each of
these three conceptions held so important a place in
the mind of the feudal class that only the most extreme
proponents of one of them ventured to create perfect
knights who conformed absolutely to a single type.
While the creators of Lancelot and Galahad sought to
produce models of courtly and religious chivalry, most
writers made a selection to suit their own tastes from
the whole mass of chivalric ideas. Thus, as we have
seen in the third chapter, Raymond Lull's picture of
the ideal knight conformed in general with ecclesiastical
views, but it contained elements from feudal chivalry
which were not in accord with the teachings of the
church. Unfortunately for the historian of chivalry few
didactic writers and still fewer romancers attempted a
complete characterization of their ideals. Each one was
inclined to confine his attention to the particular traits
which suited his purpose. As a result it is extremely
difficult to find examples which will show how the
writers of mediaeval France composed their heroes from
elements drawn from the various sets of chivalric ideas.

An interesting summary of chivalric ethics was composed by the thirteenth-century trouvère who wrote the

[26] *Le roman de la rose ou de Guillaume de Dole* (ed. G. Servois,
Société des anciens textes français, Paris, 1893), pp. 6-8.

chanson de geste, Gaydon. The author of *Gaydon* possessed more originality and imagination than most of
his contemporaries. While he observed the current literary fashions of his day, he did so with verve. Villains
who spoke scornfully of knightly customs were common
in mediaeval literature, but the peasant-born man-at-
arms who served Gaydon expressed his views with unusual vivacity. When a charming servant girl sought
his love in true courtly style, he told her to jump in a
fountain if she was too hot.[27] In another passage the
author described with rare realism the muster of a royal
host. He told of the vassals who had mortgaged their
lands to equip their levies, of the rascals of all sorts who
swarmed about in the hope of getting booty, and of
the jongleurs and prostitutes who would soon empty
the fattest purses in the army.[28] When this rather unconventional trouvère set out to describe the " traitor,"
an extremely popular character in the *chansons de geste,*
instead of penning a few brutal phrases he composed
a code of chivalry in reverse. The villain was being
dubbed a knight by his wicked episcopal uncle who
preached a sermon for the occasion.

Good nephew, listen. If you are willing to do my wishes and
commands, you will be victorious in battle. Before all else vow
to the Lord God that you will never be loyal to any man, will
never keep your faith to your liege lord, will betray and sell-out
loyal men, and will elevate the bad and abase the good. If you
take a man as your companion in arms, praise him to his face
and criticize him behind his back. Shame and make fun of
poor men, disinherit orphans, steal the dowers of widows, and
sustain murderers and thieves. Dishonor Holy Church, flee and
avoid priests and clerks, plunder completely hermits and monks,

[27] *Gaydon,* p. cix.   [28] *Ibid.,* p. lxxiii.

and beat friars. Dash little children into the mud, seize them, bite them, and if no one is looking strangle them. Punch and kick old people or at least spit in their faces. Ravage and destroy convents and allow the nuns to be raped. Wherever you are, lie and perjure yourself boldly.[29]

The author of *Gaydon* clearly favored the feudal type of chivalry more or less flavored with the ideas propounded by the church. Léon Gautier had a chivalric ideal of this sort in mind when he stated that " Chivalry is the Christian form of the military state; the knight is the Christian soldier." [30]

Although the author of *Gaydon* was familiar with the ideas of courtly love, their influence was not apparent in his perfect knight in reverse. For a delightful picture of a knight who would combine the virtues of courtly and religious chivalry we must turn to the counsel which Chrétien de Troyes placed in the mouth of Perceval's mother as her young son was about to set out on his adventurous travels. When he wrote his *Perceval,* Chrétien was determined to abjure the frivolities of his youth and to please his aged and pious patron, Philip of Alsace, count of Flanders. He would depict a true Christian knight. Fortunately Chrétien's courtly past and his grasp of human realities were too strong to permit him to afflict the world with a Galahad. Perceval became a Christian knight, but he remained an attractive human being. In him the virtues of courtly and religious chivalry were merged as completely as their conflicting elements would permit. As Perceval was about to set out for King Arthur's court to ask the

---

[29] *Ibid.,* pp. lxxxv; 194-5.   [30] *La chevalerie,* p. 2.

chivalrous monarch to dub him a knight, his mother gave him these words of advice.

If you find yourself near to or far from a lady who has need of aid or a disconsolate maiden, be ready to assist them if they ask you to. . . . He who does not do honor to ladies, must lose his own honor. Serve ladies and maidens if you would be honored by all. If you capture a lady, do not annoy her. Do nothing to displease her. He has much from a maiden who kisses her if she agrees to give a kiss. You will avoid greater intimacy if you wish to be guided by me. If she has a ring on her finger or a purse at her girdle and is moved by love or entreaties to give it to you, it is proper that you carry it away with you. . . . Speak with *prodomes*, associate with *prodomes*. A *prodome* does not lead astray those who bear him company. Above all I wish to beg you to go to churches and abbeys and pray to our Lord so that the world may do you honor and you may come to a good end.[31]

In a later passage the same advice was given to Perceval by his hermit uncle. " Believe in God, love God, adore God, honor wise men and women. Rise before the priest for it is a service which costs little and God loves it in truth because it comes from humility. If a maiden asks your aid, succor her; aid the widow and the orphan." [32]

Such was Chrétien de Troyes' conception of the courtly Christian knight. But Chrétien was too true an artist to allow his hero to conform completely to the ideal created for him. When the young Perceval ravished a kiss from the astounded and unwilling lips of the first maiden he met and took her ring by force, he rather distorted the intent of his mother's advice.[33] She

[31] *Der Persevalroman von Christian von Troyes* (ed. Alfons Hilka, Halle, 1932), lines 533-572.

[32] *Ibid.*, lines 6459-6467.   [33] *Ibid.*, lines 667-729.

had stipulated that the lady should be willing. Then there was the entrancing scene where Perceval's lovely hostess put on a short mantle over her chemise and went to his room in the dead of night to tell him her troubles. Awakened by the maiden's sobs, Perceval found her kneeling by the bed with her arms about his neck. " And so much courtesy did he do her that he took her between his arms and drew her towards him." After this courteous gesture, he listened to her tale of woe. When she had finished, the young man pressed rather hard on the limits set by his mother's counsel.[34]

"Dear friend " he said " Make me good cheer tonight. Comfort yourself, weep no more and draw towards me, wipe the tears from your eyes. . . . Lie with me in this bed. . . ." And she said "If it pleases you, I will do it." And he kissed her whom he held in his arms as he put her under the covers. . . . And she allowed him to kiss her. . . . So they lay all the night, one near the other, mouth to mouth, until day approached.[35]

Presumably Perceval got no more than the kiss allowed him by his mother, but the wrappings were far more delightful than those envisaged by the good lady.

We have glanced at ideals of knighthood created by the author of *Gaydon* and by Chrétien de Troyes. The former was the blend of feudal and religious chivalry which marked most of the heroes of the *chansons de geste* while the latter was a mixture of ecclesiastical and courtly ideas. There remains to be examined an even more common type of perfect knight—one who combined the virtues of feudal and courtly chivalry. At the beginning of his *Roman de la violette* Gerbert de

---

[34] *Der Percevalroman*, lines 1952-2047.
[35] *Ibid.*, lines 2047-2066.

Montreuil described the qualities possessed by " King Louis."

Once upon a time there was a king in France who was very handsome, bold, and full of prowess. He was young, intelligent, bold in arms, and helpful. He greatly honored knights and chose his counselors among the wise. He accepted advice, loved advice, and never was offended by it. He was very well educated and wise and his habits were good. He held dear ladies and maidens. Often he made them good cheer. He was very *preu* and had great renown.[36]

The description of the castellan of Coucy in the *Roman du castelain de Couci* followed the same general lines.

He was handsome, courteous, full of knowledge. Never did Gawain or Lancelot acquire more praise for feats of arms than he did in his day. He was ready to agree to everything honorable and was full of good qualities. . . . His renown was great everywhere. He knew how to compose chansons and jeux-partis. . . . Whether a war or a tournament was near at hand or far away he allowed nothing to prevent him from taking part. . . . Love had captured his eyes and made him feel its grave woes so that his heart and body witnessed that he loved loyally. . . .[37]

To these two purely imaginary conceptions of perfect knights in whom were blended feudal and courtly qualities I wish to add a brief contemporary description of Duke Louis of Bourbon. As the duke's biographer clearly considered him a model of knighthood, this account of Louis' good qualities deserves a place among descriptions of ideal knights.

[36] Gerbert de Montreuil, *Le roman de la violette* (ed. D. L. Buffum, Société des anciens textes français, Paris, 1928), pp. 5-6.
[37] Jakemes, *Le roman du castelain de Couci et de la dame de Fayel* (ed. Maurice Delbouille, Société des anciens textes français, Paris, 1936), p. 5.

He was a very handsome and gracious knight who loved
honor above all else. He was well supplied with good habits.
He was of high birth. He was a very amorous knight, first
towards God and then towards all ladies and high-born girls.
He was full of gracious words. He could not abide to be in a
place where he heard evil spoken of ladies and girls and this
quality he had all his life. His virtues were so agreeable to the
queen of England and to all the ladies, knights, and squires
of that realm that he was allowed (while a hostage) to go where
he willed in the kingdom. . . . Throughout the realm of
England the ladies, girls, knights, and squires called him the
king of honor and gentility.[38]

The emphasis on courtly virtues which marks this passage can be explained in part by the context—the author
was saying why Duke Louis was liked by the English
queen. As we have seen in the chapter on feudal
chivalry, the duke was noted for his prowess and devoted
himself to exercising it. Nevertheless throughout the
chronicle the author continually mentioned his hero's
courteous qualities. The picture he drew of Duke Louis
as an ideal knight was a pleasant blend of feudal and
courtly chivalry.

My picture of chivalry is now complete. The feudal
class of mediaeval France has been shown in its changing environment. Each of the three sets of chivalric
ideas and the relations between them have been examined. An attempt has been made to show the effect
of these ideas on the ethical ideals of the noblemen of
France and their possible influence on contemporary
practice. In bringing this book to an end I can only hope
that the reader has enjoyed it half as much as I have.

[38] *La chronique du bon duc Loys de Bourbon,* pp. 4-5.

INDEX